Everything the
Bible Says About

PRAYER

Everything the Bible Says About
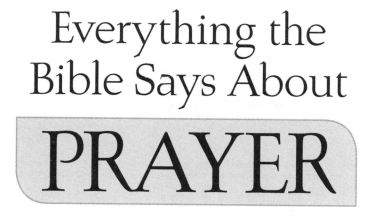
PRAYER

BETHANY HOUSE PUBLISHERS
a division of Baker Publishing Group
Minneapolis, Minnesota

Compiled by Keith Wall
Series editor: Andy McGuire

Published by Bethany House Publishers
11400 Hampshire Avenue South
Bloomington, Minnesota 55438
www.bethanyhouse.com

Bethany House Publishers is a division of
Baker Publishing Group, Grand Rapids, Michigan

Printed in the United States of America

Library of Congress Cataloging-in-Publication Data
Everything the Bible says about prayer : how do I know God hears my prayers? What should I ask for when I pray? What does God say about worshiping in prayer? How should I pray for my family? / [compiled by Keith Wall].
    p. cm.
    Summary: "A gathering of all the Bible's references to prayer, including verses on how to pray and what to pray for, what Jesus said about prayer, and examples of biblical prayers. Also provides very brief context and commentary"—Provided by publisher.
    ISBN 978-0-7642-1029-7 (pbk. : alk. paper)
    1. Prayer—Biblical teaching. 2. Bible—Quotations. I. Wall, Keith A.
BS680.P64E94 2012
248.3′2—dc23
                      2012006418

Cover design by Eric Walljasper

12 13 14 15 16 17 18   7 6 5 4 3 2 1

Contents

Introduction

Prayer: A Wish Turned Godward

Ask people to describe what prayer is, and you're likely to hear a variety of perspectives:

- Communication between the heavenly Father and his child
- A cry for help to the mighty Creator
- An expression of praise and worship to the King of Kings
- A call for guidance during fearful, confusing times

All of those responses are absolutely true and legitimate. Prayer is many things, multifaceted and nuanced. Yet prayer need not be viewed as a mysterious ritual practiced by religious professionals or super-spiritual individuals. Prayer is, at its essence, talking and listening to God. Children of God can open their hearts to him, sharing their innermost hopes and heartaches, dreads and delights. What's more, they can become attuned to what he has to say, whether as forceful as a thunderclap or as hushed as a still, small voice.

The author and hymn writer Phillips Brooks once said, "A prayer in its simplest definition is merely a wish turned Godward." It's good to be reminded that prayer doesn't need to be complicated or arduous, despite the misguided claims of some people. Most of us have no problem with the first part of Brooks's equation—forming a wish. In fact, we could recite our wish list without giving it much thought: we might wish for steady employment, the healing of a sick loved one, safety for a child, a broken relationship to be mended, financial stability, and on and on.

But wishes alone aren't much good; they're just unfulfilled yearnings and longings. That's why the second part of the equation—turning Godward—is essential to the process. Taking our wishes (and fears and heartaches) to God transforms wishful thinking and elusive hopes into powerful prayer. Through prayer to the living God, our *hope* for forgiveness becomes a fact. Our *longing* for grace is guaranteed. Our *desire* for a relationship with him becomes reality.

In the pages that follow, you'll find hundreds of Scripture verses that describe, in many different ways, what it means to turn Godward with our wishes. You'll find reasons to have confidence in the efficacy of prayer, examples of how our Christian forebears approached God, Jesus' teaching on the subject, and assurances that your prayers are heard and answered. It's likely you'll also find that your faith is fortified and your belief bolstered—faith and belief in a loving, living God who cares deeply about each and every prayer you bring to him.

Confident Before the King

Praying With Boldness

One of the few times Jesus rebuked his disciples was when they attempted to keep a group of small children from reaching him (Matthew 19:13–14). It isn't hard to see why they might have thought this was a good idea. Surely the Lord had important things on his mind and shouldn't be bothered by a mob of clamoring kids on his lap. Children are frequently loud, unruly, and terribly demanding. They know what they want and when they want it—*now!*

And yet, in correcting his well-meaning followers, Jesus gave us valuable insight into exactly what bothers God and what doesn't. According to him, children—in all their child-like exuberance—are a model for us all. *Go ahead,* God says, *climb on my lap and bother me! Ask me for what you want*

9

*and need. Know that my love is so deep that I'll never turn
you away. That's the way into the kingdom of heaven.*

If you still have your doubts, read and reflect on the following verses. By the time you are finished, the next time you pray you'll be ready to jump boldly into your Father's arms.

Listen to my cry for help, my King and my God,
    for I pray to no one but you. (**PSALM 5:2 NLT**)

To you, O LORD, I lift up my soul.
O my God, in you I trust;
    let me not be put to shame;
    let not my enemies exult over me.
Indeed, none who wait for you shall be put to
    shame;
    they shall be ashamed who are wantonly
    treacherous. (**PSALM 25:1-3 ESV**)

Come and hear, all you who fear God;
    let me tell you what he has done for me.
I cried out to him with my mouth;
    his praise was on my tongue.
If I had cherished sin in my heart,
    the Lord would not have listened;
but God has surely listened
    and has heard my prayer.
Praise be to God,
    who has not rejected my prayer
    or withheld his love from me! (**PSALM 66:16-20
NIV**)

You are my hope, O Almighty LORD.
You have been my confidence ever since I was
    young.
I depended on you before I was born. **(PSALM
71:5–6 GOD'S WORD)**

Seek the LORD while you can find him.
    Call on him now while he is near. **(ISAIAH 55:6
NLT)**

Then children were brought to him that he might lay his hands
on them and pray. The disciples rebuked the people, but Jesus
said, "Let the little children come to me and do not hinder
them, for to such belongs the kingdom of heaven." And he
laid his hands on them and went away. **(MATTHEW 19:13–14 ESV)**

*A Syrophoenician woman boldly approached Jesus and her daughter
was healed:*

He got up and departed from there to the region of Tyre and
Sidon. He entered a house and did not want anyone to know
it, but He could not escape notice. Instead, immediately after
hearing about Him, a woman whose little daughter had an
unclean spirit came and fell at His feet. Now the woman was
Greek, a Syrophoenician by birth, and she kept asking Him to
drive the demon out of her daughter. He said to her, "Allow
the children to be satisfied first, because it isn't right to take
the children's bread and throw it to the dogs."

But she replied to Him, "Lord, even the dogs under the
table eat the children's crumbs."

Then He told her, "Because of this reply, you may go. The demon has gone out of your daughter." When she went back to her home, she found her child lying on the bed, and the demon was gone. (MARK 7:24–30 HCSB)

Luke shared this example of a man who boldly asked Jesus to heal him:

As Jesus approached Jericho, a blind man was sitting by the roadside begging. When he heard the crowd going by, he asked what was happening. They told him, "Jesus of Nazareth is passing by."

He called out, "Jesus, Son of David, have mercy on me!"

Those who led the way rebuked him and told him to be quiet, but he shouted all the more, "Son of David, have mercy on me!"

Jesus stopped and ordered the man to be brought to him. When he came near, Jesus asked him, "What do you want me to do for you?"

"Lord, I want to see," he replied.

Jesus said to him, "Receive your sight; your faith has healed you." Immediately he received his sight and followed Jesus, praising God. When all the people saw it, they also praised God. (LUKE 18:35–43 NIV)

For those who are led by the Spirit of God are the children of God. The Spirit you received does not make you slaves, so that you live in fear again; rather, the Spirit you received brought about your adoption to sonship. And by him we cry, "*Abba,* Father." The Spirit himself testifies with our spirit that we are God's children. (ROMANS 8:14–16 NIV)

In the same way the Spirit also helps our weakness; for we do not know how to pray as we should, but the Spirit Himself intercedes for us with groanings too deep for words. (**ROMANS 8:26 NASB**)

[Jesus] came and preached peace to you who were far off and peace to those who were near. For through him we both have access in one Spirit to the Father. So then you are no longer strangers and aliens, but you are fellow citizens with the saints and members of the household of God. (**EPHESIANS 2:17–19 ESV**)

Because of Christ and our faith in him, we can now come boldly and confidently into God's presence. (**EPHESIANS 3:12 NLT**)

Let us then approach God's throne of grace with confidence, so that we may receive mercy and find grace to help us in our time of need. (**HEBREWS 4:16 NIV**)

And so, dear brothers and sisters, we can boldly enter heaven's Most Holy Place because of the blood of Jesus. By his death, Jesus opened a new and life-giving way through the curtain into the Most Holy Place. And since we have a great High Priest who rules over God's house, let us go right into the presence of God with sincere hearts fully trusting him. For our guilty consciences have been sprinkled with Christ's blood to make us clean, and our bodies have been washed with pure water. (**HEBREWS 10:19–22 NLT**)

Now faith is confidence in what we hope for and assurance about what we do not see. (**HEBREWS 11:1 NIV**)

Dear friends, if our conscience doesn't condemn us, we can boldly look to God and receive from him anything we ask. (1 JOHN 3:21–22 GOD'S WORD)

And this is the confidence that we have toward him, that if we ask anything according to his will he hears us. And if we know that he hears us in whatever we ask, we know that we have the requests that we have asked of him. (1 JOHN 5:14–15 ESV)

He came to the One Seated on the Throne and took the scroll from his right hand. The moment he took the scroll, the Four Animals and Twenty-four Elders fell down and worshiped the Lamb. Each had a harp and each had a bowl, a gold bowl filled with incense, the prayers of God's holy people. (REVELATION 5:7–8 THE MESSAGE)

Key Ingredients

Elements of Effective Prayer

God never intended prayer to be a recipe—a formula to follow or a perfunctory procedure to perform. That would go against the Father's desire for genuine, heartfelt communication with his children.

But while prayer is not a recipe, there are certain "key ingredients" we should all strive to include for our spiritual experience to be optimal and effective. Scripture encourages us to combine equal parts of the following:

- Humility and confession
- Thanksgiving and praise
- Pure motives and a clean heart

- Consistency and devotion
- Faith that God loves you and listens when you pray

Add in a dash of boldness and a pinch of persistence—and then expect the very best from your heavenly Father.

PRAY WITH HUMILITY

If my people, who are called by my name, will humble themselves and pray and seek my face and turn from their wicked ways, then I will hear from heaven, and I will forgive their sin. **(2 CHRONICLES 7:14 NIV)**

The LORD spoke to Manasseh and his people, but they ignored all his warnings. So the LORD sent the commanders of the Assyrian armies, and they took Manasseh prisoner. They put a ring through his nose, bound him in bronze chains, and led him away to Babylon. But while in deep distress, Manasseh sought the LORD his God and sincerely humbled himself before the God of his ancestors. And when he prayed, the LORD listened to him and was moved by his request. So the LORD brought Manasseh back to Jerusalem and to his kingdom. Then Manasseh finally realized that the LORD alone is God! **(2 CHRONICLES 33:10–13 NLT)**

> *King Manasseh ranks high among the evil rulers described in Scripture. He worshiped idols, desecrated the temple, and even sacrificed his own children. But his prayers, offered in humility, and his recognition of God's authority prompted the Lord to forgive and respond with compassion.*

God has no use for the prayers
of the people who won't listen to him.
(PROVERBS 28:9 THE MESSAGE)

Don't shoot off your mouth, or speak before you
think.
Don't be too quick to tell God what you think he
wants to hear.
God's in charge, not you—the less you speak,
the better. (ECCLESIASTES 5:2 THE MESSAGE)

Pray With Faith

And Jesus answered them, "Truly, I say to you, if you have faith and do not doubt, you will not only do what has been done to the fig tree, but even if you say to this mountain, 'Be taken up and thrown into the sea,' it will happen. And whatever you ask in prayer, you will receive, if you have faith." (MATTHEW 21:21–22 ESV)

Therefore I tell you, whatever you ask in prayer, believe that you have received it, and it will be yours. (MARK 11:24 ESV)

If you need wisdom, ask our generous God, and he will give it to you. He will not rebuke you for asking. But when you ask him, be sure that your faith is in God alone. Do not waver, for a person with divided loyalty is as unsettled as a wave of the sea that is blown and tossed by the wind. Such people should not expect to receive anything from the Lord. Their loyalty is divided between God and the world, and they are unstable in everything they do. (JAMES 1:5-8 NLT)

––––––––––––––– PRAY WITH CONSISTENCY –––––––––––––––

In [Daniel's] upper room, with his windows open toward Jerusalem, he knelt down on his knees three times that day, and prayed and gave thanks before his God, as was his custom since early days. (DANIEL 6:10 NKJV)

But the news about [Jesus] was spreading even farther, and large crowds were gathering to hear Him and to be healed of their sicknesses. But Jesus Himself would often slip away to the wilderness and pray. (LUKE 5:15–16 NASB)

All these with one accord were devoting themselves to prayer, together with the women and Mary the mother of Jesus, and his brothers. (ACTS 1:14 ESV)

Rejoice always, pray continually, give thanks in all circumstances; for this is God's will for you in Christ Jesus. (1 THESSALONIANS 5:16–18 NIV)

Now a true widow, a woman who is truly alone in this world, has placed her hope in God. She prays night and day, asking God for his help. (1 TIMOTHY 5:5 NLT)

––––––– PRAY WITH DEVOTION AND PURPOSEFULNESS –––––––

[Jesus] went up on a mountainside by himself to pray. (MATTHEW 14:23 NIV)

It was at this time that He went off to the mountain to pray, and He spent the whole night in prayer to God. (LUKE 6:12 NASB)

That evening after sunset the people brought to Jesus all the sick and demon-possessed. The whole town gathered at the door, and Jesus healed many who had various diseases. . . . Very early in the morning, while it was still dark, Jesus got up, left the house and went off to a solitary place, where he prayed. Simon and his companions went to look for him, and when they found him, they exclaimed: "Everyone is looking for you!" (MARK 1:32–37 NIV)

And with many other words [Peter] bore witness and continued to exhort them, saying, "Save yourselves from this crooked generation." So those who received his word were baptized, and there were added that day about three thousand souls. And they devoted themselves to the apostles' teaching and the fellowship, to the breaking of bread and the prayers. And awe came upon every soul, and many wonders and signs were being done through the apostles. (ACTS 2:40–43 ESV)

So the twelve summoned the congregation of the disciples and said, "It is not desirable for us to neglect the word of God in order to serve tables. Therefore, brethren, select from among you seven men of good reputation, full of the Spirit and of wisdom, whom we may put in charge of this task. But we will devote ourselves to prayer and to the ministry of the word." (ACTS 6:2–4 NASB)

Devote yourselves to prayer, being watchful and thankful.
(COLOSSIANS 4:2 NIV)

———— PRAY WITH A PURE AND RIGHTEOUS HEART ————

The LORD detests the sacrifice of the wicked,
but he delights in the prayers of the upright.
(PROVERBS 15:8 NLT)

God keeps his distance from the wicked;
he closely attends to the prayers of God-loyal
people. (PROVERBS 15:29 THE MESSAGE)

There's nothing wrong with God; the wrong is
in you.
Your wrongheaded lives caused the split between you and God.
Your sins got between you so that he doesn't
hear. (ISAIAH 59:2 THE MESSAGE)

Now we know that God does not hear sinners; but if anyone is a worshiper of God and does His will, He hears him.
(JOHN 9:31 NKJV)

I desire then that in every place the men should pray, lifting
holy hands without anger or quarreling (1 TIMOTHY 2:8 ESV)

Flee the evil desires of youth and pursue righteousness, faith,
love and peace, along with those who call on the Lord out of
a pure heart. (2 TIMOTHY 2:22 NIV)

While he lived on earth, anticipating death, Jesus cried out in pain and wept in sorrow as he offered up priestly prayers to God. Because he honored God, God answered him. (HEBREWS 5:7 THE MESSAGE)

You ask and do not receive, because you ask with wrong motives, so that you may spend it on your pleasures. (JAMES 4:3 NASB)

The urgent request of a righteous person is very powerful in its effect. Elijah was a man with a nature like ours; yet he prayed earnestly that it would not rain, and for three years and six months it did not rain on the land. Then he prayed again, and the sky gave rain and the land produced its fruit. (JAMES 5:16–18 HCSB)

My dear friends, if our hearts do not make us feel guilty, we can come without fear into God's presence. And God gives us what we ask for because we obey God's commands and do what pleases him. (1 JOHN 3:21–22 NCV)

You husbands in the same way, live with your wives in an understanding way, as with someone weaker, since she is a woman; and show her honor as a fellow heir of the grace of life, so that your prayers will not be hindered. (1 PETER 3:7 NASB)

——————— PRAY WITH THANKSGIVING ———————

[Jesus] directed the people to sit down on the ground; and He took the seven loaves and the fish; and giving thanks, He broke them and started giving them to the disciples, and the disciples gave them to the people. (MATTHEW 15:35–36 NASB)

In our prayers for you we always thank God, the Father of our Lord Jesus Christ, because we have heard about the faith you have in Christ Jesus and the love you have for all of God's people. (COLOSSIANS 1:3–4 NCV)

And let the peace of the Messiah, to which you were also called in one body, control your hearts. Be thankful. Let the message about the Messiah dwell richly among you, teaching and admonishing one another in all wisdom, and singing psalms, hymns, and spiritual songs, with gratitude in your hearts to God. And whatever you do, in word or in deed, do everything in the name of the Lord Jesus, giving thanks to God the Father through Him. (COLOSSIANS 3:15–17 HCSB)

First of all, then, I urge that supplications, prayers, intercessions, and thanksgivings be made for all people. (1 TIMOTHY 2:1 ESV)

Count on It

God Hears and Answers Your Prayers

It is a general rule of conversation that you should only speak to people who are actually listening—and only ask favors of those willing and able to say yes. Anything else would seem rude, or even a little crazy.

Yet many people attempt to pray to God without any clear conviction that he is paying attention. On one hand, that is understandable. It is in the nature of our unequal relationship with an omnipotent Creator for dialogue with him to feel a bit one-sided. We don't all hear his voice booming from a burning bush. Still, wouldn't it be nice to know *for sure* that God is listening intently to every word you say to him—and that he never leaves a prayer unanswered?

Well, you are in luck, because the Bible leaves no room for doubt on the subject. Read on and see for yourself.

———

Isaac was forty years old when he took Rebekah, the daughter of Bethuel the Aramean of Paddan-aram, the sister of Laban the Aramean, to be his wife. And Isaac prayed to the LORD for his wife, because she was barren. And the LORD granted his prayer, and Rebekah his wife conceived. (GENESIS 25:20–21 ESV)

So Ahab summoned all the Israelites and gathered the prophets at Mount Carmel. Then Elijah approached all the people and said, "How long will you hesitate between two opinions? If Yahweh is God, follow Him. But if Baal, follow him." But the people didn't answer him a word.

Then Elijah said to the people, "I am the only remaining prophet of the LORD, but Baal's prophets are 450 men. Let two bulls be given to us. They are to choose one bull for themselves, cut it in pieces, and place it on the wood but not light the fire. I will prepare the other bull and place it on the wood but not light the fire. Then you call on the name of your god, and I will call on the name of Yahweh. The God who answers with fire, He is God."

All the people answered, "That sounds good."

Then Elijah said to the prophets of Baal, "Since you are so numerous, choose for yourselves one bull and prepare it first. Then call on the name of your god but don't light the fire."

So they took the bull that he gave them, prepared it, and called on the name of Baal from morning until noon, saying, "Baal, answer us!" But there was no sound; no one answered. Then they danced, hobbling around the altar they had made.

At noon Elijah mocked them. He said, "Shout loudly, for he's a god! Maybe he's thinking it over; maybe he has wandered away; or maybe he's on the road. Perhaps he's sleeping and will wake up!" They shouted loudly, and cut themselves with knives and spears, according to their custom, until blood gushed over them. All afternoon they kept on raving until the offering of the evening sacrifice, but there was no sound; no one answered, no one paid attention.

Then Elijah said to all the people, "Come near me." So all the people approached him. Then he repaired the LORD's altar that had been torn down: Elijah took 12 stones—according to the number of the tribes of the sons of Jacob, to whom the word of the LORD had come, saying, "Israel will be your name"—and he built an altar with the stones in the name of Yahweh. Then he made a trench around the altar large enough to hold about four gallons. Next, he arranged the wood, cut up the bull, and placed it on the wood. He said, "Fill four water pots with water and pour it on the offering to be burned and on the wood." Then he said, "A second time!" and they did it a second time. And then he said, "A third time!" and they did it a third time. So the water ran all around the altar; he even filled the trench with water.

At the time for offering the evening sacrifice, Elijah the prophet approached the altar and said, "Yahweh, God of Abraham, Isaac, and Israel, today let it be known that You are God in Israel and I am Your servant, and that at Your word I have done all these things. Answer me, LORD! Answer me so that this people will know that You, Yahweh, are God and that You have turned their hearts back."

Then Yahweh's fire fell and consumed the burnt offering, the wood, the stones, and the dust, and it licked up the water that was in the trench. When all the people saw it, they fell facedown and said, "Yahweh, He is God! Yahweh, He is God!" (1 KINGS 18:20–39 HCSB).

The sons of Reuben and the Gadites and the half-tribe of Manasseh, consisting of valiant men, men who bore shield and sword and shot with bow and were skillful in battle, were 44,760, who went to war. They made war against the Hagrites, Jetur, Naphish and Nodab. They were helped against them, and the Hagrites and all who were with them were given into their hand; for they cried out to God in the battle, and He answered their prayers because they trusted in Him. (1 CHRONICLES 5:18–20 NASB)

> LORD, every morning you hear my voice.
>   Every morning, I tell you what I need,
>   and I wait for your answer. (PSALM 5:3 NCV)

> May he give you the desire of your heart
>   and make all your plans succeed.
> May we shout for joy over your victory
>   and lift up our banners in the name of our God.
> May the LORD grant all your requests.
> Now this I know:
>   The LORD gives victory to his anointed.
> He answers him from his heavenly sanctuary
>   with the victorious power of his right hand.
>   (PSALM 20:4–6 NIV)

> I waited patiently for the LORD.
> He turned to me and heard my cry for help.

He pulled me out of a horrible pit,
  out of the mud and clay.
He set my feet on a rock
  and made my steps secure.
He placed a new song in my mouth,
    a song of praise to our God.
    Many will see this and worship.
    They will trust the LORD.
Blessed is the person
  who places his confidence in the LORD
    and does not rely on arrogant people
    or those who follow lies.
You have done many miraculous things, O LORD
  my God.
You have made many wonderful plans for us.
  No one compares to you!
I will tell others about your miracles,
    which are more than I can count. (PSALM 40:1-5
    GOD'S WORD)

Turn your burdens over to the LORD,
  and he will take care of you.
    He will never let the righteous person
    stumble.
But you, O God, will throw wicked people into
  the deepest pit.
    Bloodthirsty and deceitful people will not live
    out half their days.
    But I will trust you. (PSALM 55:22-23 GOD'S
    WORD)

Moses and Aaron were his priests,
Samuel among those who prayed to him.
They prayed to God and he answered them.
(PSALM 99:6 THE MESSAGE)

The LORD is righteous in all his ways
and faithful in all he does.
The LORD is near to all who call on him,
to all who call on him in truth.
He fulfills the desires of those who fear him;
he hears their cry and saves them. (PSALM
145:17–19 NIV)

When you call, the LORD will answer.
"Yes, I am here," he will quickly reply. (ISAIAH
58:9 NLT)

Surely the arm of the LORD is not too short to
save,
nor his ear too dull to hear. (ISAIAH 59:1 NIV)

I will bring that group through the fire
and make them pure.
I will refine them like silver
and purify them like gold.
They will call on my name,
and I will answer them.
I will say, "These are my people,"
and they will say, "The LORD is our God"
(ZECHARIAH 13:9 NLT).

Ask and it will be given to you; seek and you will find; knock and the door will be opened to you. (**MATTHEW 7:7** NIV)

Jesus lifted up his eyes and said, "Father, I thank you that you have heard me. I knew that you always hear me, but I said this on account of the people standing around, that they may believe that you sent me." When he had said these things, he cried out with a loud voice, "Lazarus, come out." The man who had died came out, his hands and feet bound with linen strips, and his face wrapped with a cloth. Jesus said to them, "Unbind him, and let him go" (**JOHN 11:41–44** ESV).

We can be thankful that God always hears us, just as he always heard Jesus.

And my God will meet all your needs according to the riches of his glory in Christ Jesus. (**PHILIPPIANS 4:19** NIV)

Wisdom From the Master

Jesus' Teaching on Prayer

Judging from the vast number of books written through the ages on the subject of prayer—enough to fill a library or two, no doubt—praying to God must be a deeply mysterious and complicated thing to do. Why else would we need so much advice about how to get it right? The Bible itself must be a tangle of inscrutable instruction to require that much interpretation. Right?

Not according to Jesus. What he had to say on the subject of prayer is remarkably simple, down-to-earth, and positively liberating. His life itself is a model of constant communion with God—a path he showed us how to walk as easily as he did himself.

In this section you will cut through the red tape of inherited theology and go straight to the source: the teachings of Jesus Christ, the Master of Prayer.

Beware of practicing your righteousness before men to be noticed by them; otherwise you have no reward with your Father who is in heaven.

So when you give to the poor, do not sound a trumpet before you, as the hypocrites do in the synagogues and in the streets, so that they may be honored by men. Truly I say to you, they have their reward in full. But when you give to the poor, do not let your left hand know what your right hand is doing, so that your giving will be in secret; and your Father who sees what is done in secret will reward you.

When you pray, you are not to be like the hypocrites; for they love to stand and pray in the synagogues and on the street corners so that they may be seen by men. Truly I say to you, they have their reward in full. But you, when you pray, go into your inner room, close your door and pray to your Father who is in secret, and your Father who sees what is done in secret will reward you.

And when you are praying, do not use meaningless repetition as the Gentiles do, for they suppose that they will be heard for their many words. So do not be like them; for your Father knows what you need before you ask Him.

Pray, then, in this way:

> Our Father who is in heaven,
> Hallowed be Your name.
> Your kingdom come.

Your will be done,
On earth as it is in heaven.
Give us this day our daily bread.
And forgive us our debts, as we also have for-
given our debtors.
And do not lead us into temptation, but deliver
us from evil. [For Yours is the kingdom and
the power and the glory forever. Amen.]

For if you forgive others for their transgressions, your heav-enly Father will also forgive you. But if you do not forgive others, then your Father will not forgive your transgressions. (MATTHEW 6:1–15 NASB)

If you, then, though you are evil, know how to give good gifts to your children, how much more will your Father in heaven give good gifts to those who ask him! (MATTHEW 7:11 NIV)

You have heard that it was said, "Love your neighbor and hate your enemy." But I tell you, love your enemies and pray for those who persecute you, that you may be children of your Father in heaven. (MATTHEW 5:43–45 NIV)

Jesus told his disciples, I tell you that if two of you on earth agree about something and pray for it, it will be done for you by my Father in heaven. This is true because if two or three people come together in my name, I am there with them. (MATTHEW 18:19–20 NCV)

The disciples brought to Jesus a boy afflicted by a demon.

When Jesus saw that a crowd was running to the scene, he gave an order to the evil spirit. He said, "You spirit that won't let him talk, I command you to come out of him and never enter him again."

The evil spirit screamed, shook the child violently, and came out. The boy looked as if he were dead, and everyone said, "He's dead!"

Jesus took his hand and helped him to stand up.

When Jesus went into a house, his disciples asked him privately, "Why couldn't we force the spirit out of the boy?"

He told them, "This kind of spirit can be forced out only by prayer" (MARK 9:25–29 GOD'S WORD).

Then Jesus said to them, "Suppose one of you went to your friend's house at midnight and said to him, 'Friend, loan me three loaves of bread. A friend of mine has come into town to visit me, but I have nothing for him to eat.' Your friend inside the house answers, 'Don't bother me! The door is already locked, and my children and I are in bed. I cannot get up and give you anything.' I tell you, if friendship is not enough to make him get up to give you the bread, your boldness will make him get up and give you whatever you need. So I tell you, ask, and God will give to you. Search, and you will find. Knock, and the door will open for you. Yes, everyone who asks will receive. The one who searches will find. And everyone who knocks will have the door opened. If your children ask for a fish, which of you would give them a snake instead? Or, if your children ask for an egg, would you give them a scorpion? Even though you are bad, you know how to give good things to your children. How much more your heavenly Father will give the Holy Spirit to those who ask him!" (LUKE 11:5–13 NCV).

*Telling God things is only part of prayer; listening to his voice is
equally important, as Jesus pointed out:*

I assure you: Anyone who doesn't enter the sheep pen by the
door but climbs in some other way, is a thief and a robber. The
one who enters by the door is the shepherd of the sheep. The
doorkeeper opens it for him, and the sheep hear his voice. He
calls his own sheep by name and leads them out. When he has
brought all his own outside, he goes ahead of them. The sheep
follow him because they recognize his voice. They will never
follow a stranger; instead they will run away from him, because
they don't recognize the voice of strangers. (JOHN 10:1–5 HCSB)

Very truly I tell you, whoever believes in me will do the works
I have been doing, and they will do even greater things than
these, because I am going to the Father. And I will do whatever you ask in my name, so that the Father may be glorified
in the Son. You may ask me for anything in my name, and I
will do it. (JOHN 14:12–14 NIV)

If you abide in me, and my words abide in you, ask whatever
you wish, and it will be done for you. (JOHN 15:7 ESV)

And [Jesus] taught and said to them, Is it not written, My
house shall be called a house of prayer for all the nations?
But you have turned it into a den of robbers. (MARK 11:17 AMP)

Two men went to the Temple to pray. One was a Pharisee, and
the other was a despised tax collector. The Pharisee stood by
himself and prayed this prayer: "I thank you, God, that I am
not a sinner like everyone else. For I don't cheat, I don't sin, and
I don't commit adultery. I'm certainly not like that tax collector! I fast twice a week, and I give you a tenth of my income."

But the tax collector stood at a distance and dared not even lift his eyes to heaven as he prayed. Instead, he beat his chest in sorrow, saying, "O God, be merciful to me, for I am a sinner." I tell you, this sinner, not the Pharisee, returned home justified before God. For those who exalt themselves will be humbled, and those who humble themselves will be exalted. (LUKE 18:10–14 NLT)

And he told them a parable to the effect that they ought always to pray and not lose heart. He said, "In a certain city there was a judge who neither feared God nor respected man. And there was a widow in that city who kept coming to him and saying, 'Give me justice against my adversary.' For a while he refused, but afterward he said to himself, 'Though I neither fear God nor respect man, yet because this widow keeps bothering me, I will give her justice, so that she will not beat me down by her continual coming.'" And the Lord said, "Hear what the unrighteous judge says. And will not God give justice to his elect, who cry to him day and night? Will he delay long over them? I tell you, he will give justice to them speedily" (LUKE 18:1–8 ESV).

"Have faith in God," Jesus answered. "Truly I tell you, if anyone says to this mountain, 'Go, throw yourself into the sea,' and does not doubt in their heart but believes that what they say will happen, it will be done for them. Therefore I tell you, whatever you ask for in prayer, believe that you have received it, and it will be yours. And when you stand praying, if you hold anything against anyone, forgive them, so that your Father in heaven may forgive you your sins" (MARK 11:22–25 NIV).

Divine Direction

Prayer for Guidance and Wisdom

The poet Robert Frost spoke for all of us when he wrote the famous lines:

> Two roads diverged in a yellow wood,
> And sorry I could not travel both
> And be one traveler, long I stood
> And looked down one as far as I could
> To where it bent in the undergrowth. . . .[1]

It would be hard to find a more universal human experience than this. After all, life is full of diverging roads and

1. Robert Frost, "The Road Not Taken," *Mountain Interval* (New York: Henry Holt and Company, 1920).

perplexing moments of decision. Who hasn't stood strain-
ing to see as far as possible into the future, hoping for some
insight into which of the paths before them is the right one?
Who hasn't struggled to balance competing priorities and
conflicting values?

In the end, the poet took the road "less traveled by," and for
him that choice "made all the difference." But are we left with
nothing more than random chance and raw intuition when
it is our turn to make important decisions? Not according
to the Scriptures in this section. They teach us to seek God's
guidance in prayer at all of life's crossroads. Then we will
look back and say, "I took the road God led me to, and *that*
has made all the difference."

God appeared to Solomon and said to him, "Ask for whatever
you want me to give you."

Solomon answered, "You have been very kind to my father
David, and you have made me king in his place. Now, LORD
God, may your promise to my father David come true. You
have made me king of a people who are as many as the dust
of the earth. Now give me wisdom and knowledge so I can
lead these people in the right way, because no one can rule
them without your help."

God said to Solomon, "You have not asked for wealth or
riches or honor, or for the death of your enemies, or for a
long life. But since you have asked for wisdom and knowledge
to lead my people, over whom I have made you king, I will
give you wisdom and knowledge. I will also give you more
wealth, riches, and honor than any king who has lived before
you or any who will live after you" **(2 CHRONICLES 1:7–12 NCV)**.

Because of your great compassion you did not abandon them in the wilderness. By day the pillar of cloud did not fail to guide them on their path, nor the pillar of fire by night to shine on the way they were to take. (NEHEMIAH 9:19 NIV)

David prayed to God:

> Lord, tell me your ways.
>   Show me how to live.
> Guide me in your truth,
>   and teach me, my God, my Savior.
> I trust you all day long. (PSALM 25:4–5 NCV)

> For You are my rock and my fortress;
> Therefore, for Your name's sake,
> Lead me and guide me. (PSALM 31:3 NKJV)

Moses prayed:

> Teach us to number each of our days
>   so that we may grow in wisdom. (PSALM 90:12
>   GOD'S WORD)

> Give me understanding, so that I may keep your
>   law
>   and obey it with all my heart.
> Direct me in the path of your commands,
>   for there I find delight.
> Turn my heart toward your statutes
>   and not toward selfish gain. (PSALM 119:34–36
>   NIV)

————

David said to God:

Investigate my life, O God,
    find out everything about me;
Cross-examine and test me,
    get a clear picture of what I'm about;
See for yourself whether I've done anything
        wrong—
    then guide me on the road to eternal life.
(PSALM 139:23–24 THE MESSAGE)

————

Tune your ears to wisdom,
    and concentrate on understanding.
Cry out for insight,
    and ask for understanding.
Search for them as you would for silver;
    seek them like hidden treasures.
Then you will understand what it means to fear
        the LORD,
    and you will gain knowledge of God.
For the LORD grants wisdom!
    From his mouth come knowledge and
        understanding.
    He grants a treasure of common sense to the
        honest.
    He is a shield to those who walk with
        integrity.
    He guards the paths of the just
        and protects those who are faithful to him.

Then you will understand what is right, just,
    and fair,
and you will find the right way to go.
For wisdom will enter your heart,
    and knowledge will fill you with joy.
Wise choices will watch over you.
    Understanding will keep you safe. (**PROVERBS
    2:2–11 NLT**)

Trust in the LORD with all your heart;
    do not depend on your own understanding.
Seek his will in all you do,
    and he will show you which path to take.
    (**PROVERBS 3:5–6 NLT**)

Whether you turn to the right or to the left, your ears will
hear a voice behind you, saying, "This is the way; walk in
it" (**ISAIAH 30:21 NIV**).

I will guide them on paths they have not known.
I will turn darkness to light in front of them
and rough places into level ground.
This is what I will do for them,
    and I will not forsake them. (**ISAIAH 42:16 HCSB**)

And the LORD will continually guide you,
And satisfy your desire in scorched places,
And give strength to your bones;
And you will be like a watered garden,
And like a spring of water whose waters do not
    fail. (**ISAIAH 58:11 NASB**)

> This is what the LORD says:
> Stand at the crossroads and look.
> Ask which paths are the old, reliable paths.
> Ask which way leads to blessings.
> Live that way, and find a resting place for
> yourselves. (JEREMIAH 6:16 GOD'S WORD)

The Lord said, Call to Me, and I will answer you, and show you great and mighty things, which you do not know. (JEREMIAH 33:3 NKJV)

> Let's take a good look at the way we're living
> and reorder our lives under God.
> Let's lift our hearts and hands at one and the
> same time,
> praying to God in heaven:
> "We've been contrary and willful"
> (LAMENTATIONS 3:40–42 THE MESSAGE).

> He will give light to those who live in the dark
> and in death's shadow.
> He will guide us into the way of peace. (LUKE
> 1:79 GOD'S WORD)

Make up your minds not to worry ahead of time about what you will say. I will give you the wisdom to say things that none of your enemies will be able to stand against or prove wrong. (LUKE 21:14–15 NCV)

Jesus said, But when he, the Spirit of truth, comes, he will guide you into all the truth. He will not speak on his own; he will speak only what he hears, and he will tell you what is yet to come. He will glorify me because it is from me that he will receive what he will make known to you. (JOHN 16:13–14 NIV)

I pray that the glorious Father, the God of our Lord Jesus Christ, would give you a spirit of wisdom and revelation as you come to know Christ better. (EPHESIANS 1:17 GOD'S WORD)

If any of you lacks wisdom, let him ask God, who gives generously to all without reproach, and it will be given him. (JAMES 1:5 ESV)

Finding Freedom

Prayer for Forgiveness

Of all the things we ever say to God, one simple phrase always belongs at the top of the list: *Forgive me*. Everything else we might ask for or offer up in conversation with him is moot so long as unacknowledged sin stands between us. Though God's forgiveness is already assured—paid for in full by Christ's sacrifice and ultimate triumph over death—confession is the role *we* must play in reaping the benefit of salvation.

Of course, just because something is simple doesn't mean it is easy. While a plea for forgiveness is the most important prayer you'll ever utter, it is also frequently the most difficult. Genuine repentance and contrition—necessary ingredients of true confession—don't come easily to the proud and stubborn human heart.

That's why the Bible includes ample advice, assurance, and models of confession to help us along.

—————

Give in to God, come to terms with him
and everything will turn out just fine.
Let him tell you what to do;
take his words to heart.
Come back to God Almighty
and he'll rebuild your life.
Clean house of everything evil.
Relax your grip on your money
and abandon your gold-plated luxury.
God Almighty will be your treasure,
more wealth than you can imagine.
You'll take delight in God, the Mighty One,
and look to him joyfully, boldly.
You'll pray to him and he'll listen;
he'll help you do what you've promised.
You'll decide what you want and it will
happen;
your life will be bathed in light.
To those who feel low you'll say, "Chin up! Be
brave!"
and God will save them.
Yes, even the guilty will escape,
escape through God's grace in your life. (JOB
22:21–30 THE MESSAGE)

—————

For the sake of your name, LORD,
forgive my iniquity, though it is great. . . .

Turn to me and be gracious to me,
  for I am lonely and afflicted.
Relieve the troubles of my heart
  and free me from my anguish.
Look on my affliction and my distress
  and take away all my sins. (PSALM 25:11, 16–18
    NIV)

Blessed is he whose transgression is forgiven,
Whose sin is covered.
Blessed is the man to whom the LORD does not
    impute iniquity.
And in whose spirit there is no deceit.
When I kept silent, my bones grew old
Through my groaning all the day long.
For day and night Your hand was heavy upon me;
My vitality was turned into the drought of
    summer.
I acknowledged my sin to You,
And my iniquity I have not hidden.
I said, "I will confess my transgressions to the
    LORD,"
And You forgave the iniquity of my sin. (PSALM
    32:1–5 NKJV)

Have mercy on me, O God,
  according to your unfailing love;
according to your great compassion
  blot out my transgressions.
Wash away all my iniquity
  and cleanse me from my sin.

For I know my transgressions,
　　and my sin is always before me.
Against you, you only, have I sinned
　　and done what is evil in your sight;
so you are right in your verdict
　　and justified when you judge.
Surely I was sinful at birth,
　　sinful from the time my mother conceived
　　　　me.
Yet you desired faithfulness even in the womb;
　　you taught me wisdom in that secret place.
Cleanse me with hyssop, and I will be clean;
　　wash me, and I will be whiter than snow.
Let me hear joy and gladness;
　　let the bones you have crushed rejoice.
Hide your face from my sins
　　and blot out all my iniquity.
Create in me a pure heart, O God,
　　and renew a steadfast spirit within me.
Do not cast me from your presence
　　or take your Holy Spirit from me.
Restore to me the joy of your salvation
　　and grant me a willing spirit, to sustain me.
Then I will teach transgressors your ways,
　　so that sinners will turn back to you.
Deliver me from the guilt of bloodshed, O God,
　　you who are God my Savior,
　　and my tongue will sing of your
　　　　righteousness.
Open my lips, Lord,
　　and my mouth will declare your praise.

You do not delight in sacrifice, or I would bring
    it;
you do not take pleasure in burnt offerings.
My sacrifice, O God, is a broken spirit;
    a broken and contrite heart
you, God, will not despise. **(PSALM 51:1–17 NIV)**

Help us, O God, our savior, for the glory of your
    name.
Rescue us, and forgive our sins for the honor of
    your name. **(PSALM 79:9 GOD'S WORD)**

The LORD is merciful and gracious,
Slow to anger, and abounding in mercy.
He will not always strive with us,
Nor will He keep His anger forever.
He has not dealt with us according to our sins,
Nor punished us according to our iniquities.
For as the heavens are high above the earth,
So great is His mercy toward those who fear
    Him;
As far as the east is from the west,
So far has He removed our transgressions from
    us. **(PSALM 103:8–12 NKJV)**

Now therefore, our God, hear the prayer of Your servant, and his supplications, and for the Lord's sake cause Your face to shine on Your sanctuary, which is desolate. O my God, incline Your ear and hear; open Your eyes and see our desolations, and the city which is called by Your name; for we do not present our supplications before You because of our righteous deeds, but because of Your great mercies. O Lord, hear! O Lord, forgive! O Lord, listen and act! Do not delay for Your own sake, my God, for Your city and Your people are called by Your name. (DANIEL 9:17–19 NKJV)

Who is a God like You,
removing iniquity and passing over rebellion
for the remnant of His inheritance?
He does not hold on to His anger forever,
because He delights in faithful love.
He will again have compassion on us;
He will vanquish our iniquities.
You will cast all our sins
into the depths of the sea. (MICAH 7:18–19 HCSB)

Maybe the family of Judah will hear what disasters I am planning to bring on them and will stop doing wicked things. Then I would forgive them for the sins and the evil things they have done. (JEREMIAH 36:3 NCV)

Forgive us our sins,
as we have forgiven those who sin against us.
(MATTHEW 6:12 NLT)

Whenever you pray, forgive anything you have against anyone. Then your Father in heaven will forgive your failures. (MARK 11:25 GOD'S WORD)

The tax collector stood at a distance. He would not even look up to heaven, but beat his breast and said, "God, have mercy on me, a sinner" (LUKE 18:13 NIV).

Come back to God, and he will forgive your sins. Then the Lord will send the time of rest. (ACTS 3:19 NCV)

Paul recounted his encounter with God on the road to Damascus:

Then [Ananias] told me, "The God of our ancestors has chosen you to know his will and to see the Righteous One and hear him speak. For you are to be his witness, telling everyone what you have seen and heard. What are you waiting for? Get up and be baptized. Have your sins washed away by calling on the name of the Lord" (ACTS 22:14-16 NLT).

Confess your sins to each other and pray for each other so that you can live together whole and healed. The prayer of a person living right with God is something powerful to be reckoned with. (JAMES 5:16 THE MESSAGE)

If we confess our sins, he is faithful and just to forgive us our sins and to cleanse us from all unrighteousness. (1 JOHN 1:9 ESV)

Let Righteousness Reign

Prayer for Salvation and Justice

If you want to know what a heartfelt plea for justice sounds like, open your Bible to nearly any of the psalms. David—first as a fugitive and rebel, and then as the king of an unruly nation—was never shy about asking God to deliver him from his enemies and give them what they richly deserved, often in graphic detail.

Then Jesus came and introduced a new and radical perspective on justice. "Love your enemies and pray for those who persecute you," he said. "If someone strikes you on one cheek, offer them the other as well" (see Matthew 5:39). Though we are still free to ask God for help in bringing an end to unjust circumstances in our own lives, Jesus broadened our horizons by challenging us to also intercede for our enemies. We are called to pray that *all* people would come to faith in Christ, and we are to do everything we can to lead them to God. We are to pray for others' salvation, and often the answer to those prayers includes our own actions: sharing the truth about God.

Scripture is filled with both aspects of God's will—his will that all people come to him and receive his forgiveness, and his will that justice be carried out in his own way and in his own time. That's God's job; our job is to pray diligently for the salvation of others and the just treatment for all, good and bad alike.

***

At the dedication of the temple, Solomon prayed for God's justice:

And let these words that I've prayed in the presence of GOD be always right there before him, day and night, so that he'll do what is right for me, to guarantee justice for his people Israel day after day after day. Then all the people on earth will know GOD is the true God; there is no other God. And you, your lives must be totally obedient to GOD, our personal God, following the life path he has cleared, alert and attentive to everything he has made plain this day. **(1 KINGS 8:59–61 THE MESSAGE)**

In the midst of Job's hardship, Elihu pointed out that God listens when people call out to him and responds justly.

People cry out when they are oppressed.
They groan beneath the power of the mighty.
Yet they don't ask, "Where is God my Creator,
the one who gives songs in the night?

Where is the one who makes us smarter than the
    animals
  and wiser than the birds of the sky?"
And when they cry out, God does not answer
  because of their pride.
But it is wrong to say God doesn't listen,
  to say the Almighty isn't concerned.
You say you can't see him,
  but he will bring justice if you will only wait.
You say he does not respond to sinners with
    anger
  and is not greatly concerned about
    wickedness.
But you are talking nonsense, Job.
  You have spoken like a fool. (JOB 35:9–16 NLT)

LORD, hear me begging for fairness;
  listen to my cry for help.
Pay attention to my prayer,
  because I speak the truth.
You will judge that I am right;
  your eyes can see what is true.
You have examined my heart;
  you have tested me all night.
You questioned me without finding anything
    wrong;
  I have not sinned with my mouth.
I have obeyed your commands,
  so I have not done what evil people do.
I have done what you told me;
  I have not failed.

I call to you, God,
  and you answer me.
Listen to me now,
  and hear what I say.
Your love is wonderful.
  By your power you save those who trust you
  from their enemies.
Protect me as you would protect your own eye.
  Hide me under the shadow of your wings.
Keep me from the wicked who attack me,
  from my enemies who surround me.
They are selfish
  and brag about themselves.
They have chased me until they have surrounded
    me.
  They plan to throw me to the ground.
They are like lions ready to kill;
  like lions, they sit in hiding.
Lord, rise up, face the enemy, and throw them
    down.
  Save me from the wicked with your sword.
    (PSALM 17:1–13 NCV)

I call out at the top of my lungs,
  "GOD! Answer! I'll do whatever you say."
I called to you, "Save me
  so I can carry out all your instructions."
I was up before sunrise,
  crying for help, hoping for a word from you.
I stayed awake all night,
  prayerfully pondering your promise.

In your love, listen to me;
   in your justice, GOD, keep me alive.
As those out to get me come closer and closer,
   they go farther and farther from the truth you
      reveal;
But you're the closest of all to me, GOD,
   and all your judgments true.
I've known all along from the evidence of your
      words
   that you meant them to last forever. (PSALM
      119:145–152 THE MESSAGE)

————————

The Lord said,

Quit your worship charades.
   I can't stand your trivial religious games:
Monthly conferences, weekly Sabbaths, special
      meetings—
   meetings, meetings, meetings—I can't stand
      one more!
Meetings for this, meetings for that. I hate them!
   You've worn me out!
I'm sick of your religion, religion, religion,
   while you go right on sinning.
When you put on your next prayer-performance,
   I'll be looking the other way.
No matter how long or loud or often you pray,
   I'll not be listening.
And do you know why? Because you've been
      tearing
   people to pieces, and your hands are bloody.

Go home and wash up.
    Clean up your act.
Sweep your lives clean of your evildoings
    so I don't have to look at them any longer.
Say no to wrong.
    Learn to do good.
Work for justice.
    Help the down-and-out.
Stand up for the homeless.
    Go to bat for the defenseless. (ISAIAH 1:13–17
      THE MESSAGE)

I am God,
    the one and only.
I don't just talk to myself
    or mumble under my breath.
I never told Jacob,
    "Seek me in emptiness, in dark nothingness."
I am God. I work out in the open,
    saying what's right, setting things right.
    (ISAIAH 45:18–19 THE MESSAGE)

I know, God, that mere mortals
    can't run their own lives,
That men and women
    don't have what it takes to take charge of life.
So correct us, God, as you see best.
    Don't lose your temper. That would be the
      end of us.
Vent your anger on the godless nations,
    who refuse to acknowledge you,

And on the people
who won't pray to you. (JEREMIAH 10:23–25 THE
MESSAGE)

*When Jeremiah's enemies plotted against him, the prophet cried
out to God,*

Pay attention to me, LORD.
Hear what my opponents are saying!
Should good be repaid with evil?
Yet they have dug a pit for me.
Remember how I stood before You
to speak good on their behalf,
to turn Your anger from them.
Therefore, hand their children over to famine,
and pour the sword's power on them.
Let their wives become childless and widowed,
their husbands slain by deadly disease,
their young men struck down by the sword in
        battle.
Let a cry be heard from their houses
when You suddenly bring raiders against them,
for they have dug a pit to capture me
and have hidden snares for my feet.
But You, LORD, know
all their deadly plots against me.
Do not wipe out their guilt;
do not blot out their sin before You.
Let them be forced to stumble before You;
deal with them in the time of Your anger.
        (JEREMIAH 18:19–23 HCSB)

I called out your name, O God,
  called from the bottom of the pit.
You listened when I called out, "Don't shut your
    ears!
  Get me out of here! Save me!"
You came close when I called out.
  You said, "It's going to be all right."
You took my side, Master;
  you brought me back alive!
God, you saw the wrongs heaped on me.
  Give me my day in court!
Yes, you saw their mean-minded schemes,
  their plots to destroy me.
You heard, God, their vicious gossip,
  their behind-my-back plots to ruin me.
They never quit, these enemies of mine, dream-
    ing up mischief,
  hatching out malice, day after day after day.
Sitting down or standing up—just look at them!—
  they mock me with vulgar doggerel.
Make them pay for what they've done, God.
  Give them their just deserts.
Break their miserable hearts!
  Damn their eyes!
Get good and angry. Hunt them down.
  Make a total demolition here under your
    heaven! (LAMENTATIONS 3:55–66 THE
    MESSAGE)

Then Jesus went to all the towns and villages, teaching in
their synagogues, preaching the good news of the kingdom,

and healing every disease and every sickness. When He saw the crowds, He felt compassion for them, because they were weary and worn out, like sheep without a shepherd. Then He said to His disciples, "The harvest is abundant, but the workers are few. Therefore, pray to the Lord of the harvest to send out workers into His harvest." (MATTHEW 9:35–39 HCSB)

Love your enemies, do good to those who hate you, bless those who curse you, pray for those who mistreat you. (LUKE 6:27–28 NIV)

Brothers and sisters, my heart's desire and prayer to God for the Israelites is that they may be saved. (ROMANS 10:1 NIV)

Dear brothers and sisters, I urge you in the name of our Lord Jesus Christ to join in my struggle by praying to God for me. Do this because of your love for me, given to you by the Holy Spirit. Pray that I will be rescued from those in Judea who refuse to obey God. Pray also that the believers there will be willing to accept the donation I am taking to Jerusalem. (ROMANS 15:30–31 NLT)

Pray in the Spirit at all times and on every occasion. Stay alert and be persistent in your prayers for all believers everywhere. And pray for me, too. Ask God to give me the right words so I can boldly explain God's mysterious plan that the Good News is for Jews and Gentiles alike. (EPHESIANS 6:18–19 NLT)

Pray for us that God will give us an opportunity to tell people his message. Pray that we can preach the secret that God has made known about Christ. This is why I am in prison. Pray

that I can speak in a way that will make it clear, as I should.
(COLOSSIANS 4:3-4 NCV)

And now, brothers and sisters, pray for us that the Lord's teaching will continue to spread quickly and that people will give honor to that teaching, just as happened with you. And pray that we will be protected from stubborn and evil people, because not all people believe.

But the Lord is faithful and will give you strength and will protect you from the Evil One. The Lord makes us feel sure that you are doing and will continue to do the things we told you. May the Lord lead your hearts into God's love and Christ's patience. (2 THESSALONIANS 3:1-5 NCV)

I urge, then, first of all, that petitions, prayers, intercession and thanksgiving be made for all people—for kings and all those in authority, that we may live peaceful and quiet lives in all godliness and holiness. This is good, and pleases God our Savior, who wants all people to be saved and to come to a knowledge of the truth. (1 TIMOTHY 2:1-4 NIV)

A Mighty Fortress

Prayer for Protection

For centuries, humans wouldn't dream of stepping into harm's way without first praying for God's protection. In fact, it is easy to imagine that the very first prayers we uttered after leaving Eden were cries for divine shelter from harm. Sometimes those prayers went on for hours or days in the form of ceremonial blessings—when embarking on a sea voyage, on the eve of battle, or before any dangerous undertaking. Those left behind to wait probably came close to praying "without ceasing" until their loved ones were safely home again. That's because we instinctively know that our survival is not just a matter of intelligence, skill, or luck. We *need* God's protective covering to succeed in life's riskier endeavors.

These days it is tempting to trust in technology or worldly wealth and authority to protect us when we need it most. The verses that follow are a necessary reminder to make God our sole source of protection—and to call on him alone in troubled times.

Now Moses sent messengers from Kadesh to the king of Edom. "Thus says your brother Israel: 'You know all the hardship that has befallen us, how our fathers went down to Egypt, and we dwelt in Egypt a long time, and the Egyptians afflicted us and our fathers. When we cried out to the LORD, He heard our voice and sent the Angel and brought us up out of Egypt; now here we are in Kadesh, a city on the edge of your border'" (NUMBERS 20:14–16 NKJV).

Then Samuel said, "Assemble all Israel at Mizpah, and I will intercede with the LORD for you." When they had assembled at Mizpah, they drew water and poured it out before the LORD. On that day they fasted and there they confessed, "We have sinned against the LORD." Now Samuel was serving as leader of Israel at Mizpah.

When the Philistines heard that Israel had assembled at Mizpah, the rulers of the Philistines came up to attack them. When the Israelites heard of it, they were afraid because of the Philistines. They said to Samuel, "Do not stop crying out to the LORD our God for us, that he may rescue us from the hand of the Philistines." Then Samuel took a suckling lamb and sacrificed it as a whole burnt offering to the LORD. He cried out to the LORD on Israel's behalf, and the LORD answered him.

While Samuel was sacrificing the burnt offering, the Philistines drew near to engage Israel in battle. But that day the LORD thundered with loud thunder against the Philistines and threw them into such a panic that they were routed before the Israelites. **(1 SAMUEL 7:5–10 NIV)**

David sang to the LORD the words of this song when the LORD delivered him from the hand of all his enemies and from the hand of Saul. He said:

> The LORD is my rock, my fortress and my
>   deliverer;
>   my God is my rock, in whom I take refuge,
>   my shield and the horn of my salvation.
> He is my stronghold, my refuge and my savior—
>   from violent people you save me.
> I called to the LORD, who is worthy of praise,
>   and have been saved from my enemies.
> The waves of death swirled about me;
>   the torrents of destruction overwhelmed me.
> The cords of the grave coiled around me;
>   the snares of death confronted me.
> In my distress I called to the LORD;
>   I called out to my God.
> From his temple he heard my voice;
>   my cry came to his ears. **(2 SAMUEL 22:1–7 NIV)**

> The LORD is my shepherd;
> I shall not want.
> He makes me to lie down in green pastures;
> He leads me beside the still waters.

He restores my soul;
He leads me in the paths of righteousness
For His name's sake.
Yea, though I walk through the valley of the
    shadow of death,
I will fear no evil;
For You are with me;
Your rod and Your staff, they comfort me.
You prepare a table before me in the presence of
    my enemies;
You anoint my head with oil;
My cup runs over.
Surely goodness and mercy shall follow me
All the days of my life;
And I will dwell in the house of the LORD
Forever. **(PSALM 23 NKJV)**

LORD, I give myself to you.
my God, I trust you.
Do not let me be disgraced;
    do not let my enemies laugh at me.
No one who trusts you will be disgraced,
    but those who sin without excuse will be dis-
        graced. **(PSALM 25:1–3 NCV)**

When I was desperate, I called out,
and GOD got me out of a tight spot.
GOD's angel sets up a circle
of protection around us while we pray. . . .
GOD keeps an eye on his friends,
his ears pick up every moan and groan.

GOD won't put up with rebels;
he'll cull them from the pack.
Is anyone crying for help? GOD is listening,
ready to rescue you. (PSALM 34:6-7, 15-17 THE
   MESSAGE)

I wait quietly before God,
   for my victory comes from him.
He alone is my rock and my salvation,
   my fortress where I will never be shaken. . . .
Let all that I am wait quietly before God,
   for my hope is in him.
He alone is my rock and my salvation,
   my fortress where I will not be shaken.
My victory and honor come from God alone.
   He is my refuge, a rock where no enemy can
      reach me.
O my people, trust in him at all times.
   Pour out your heart to him,
   for God is our refuge. (PSALM 62:1-2, 5-8 NLT)

I love God because he listened to me,
   listened as I begged for mercy.
He listened so intently
   as I laid out my case before him.
Death stared me in the face,
   hell was hard on my heels.
Up against it, I didn't know which way to turn;
   then I called out to GOD for help:
"Please, GOD!" I cried out.
   "Save my life!"

GOD is gracious—it is he who makes things
    right,
our most compassionate God.
GOD takes the side of the helpless;
    when I was at the end of my rope, he saved
    me. (PSALM 116:1–6 THE MESSAGE)

The Lord says,

Because you love me, I will rescue you.
    I will protect you because you know my name.
When you call to me, I will answer you.
    I will be with you when you are in trouble.
I will save you and honor you.
I will satisfy you with a long life.
    I will show you how I will save you. (PSALM
    91:14–16 GOD'S WORD)

When Jonah tried to avoid God's instructions to go and preach in Nineveh, he temporarily took refuge on a ship. God sent a storm to stop the ship.

Then the [sailors] were even more afraid and said to [Jonah], "What is this you've done?" The men knew he was fleeing from the LORD's presence, because he had told them. So they said to him, "What should we do to you to calm this sea that's against us?" For the sea was getting worse and worse.

He answered them, "Pick me up and throw me into the sea so it may quiet down for you, for I know that I'm to blame for this violent storm that is against you." Nevertheless, the men rowed hard to get back to dry land, but they couldn't because the sea was raging against them more and more.

So they called out to the LORD: "Please, Yahweh, don't let us perish because of this man's life, and don't charge us with innocent blood! For You, Yahweh, have done just as You pleased." Then they picked up Jonah and threw him into the sea, and the sea stopped its raging. (JONAH 1:10–15 HCSB)

And [Jesus] went a little beyond them, and fell on His face and prayed, saying, "My Father, if it is possible, let this cup pass from Me; yet not as I will, but as You will." And He came to the disciples and found them sleeping, and said to Peter, "So, you men could not keep watch with Me for one hour? Keep watching and praying that you may not enter into temptation; the spirit is willing, but the flesh is weak" (MATTHEW 26:39–41 NASB).

Jesus said, Be careful not to spend your time feasting, drinking, or worrying about worldly things. If you do, that day might come on you suddenly, like a trap on all people on earth. So be ready all the time. Pray that you will be strong enough to escape all these things that will happen and that you will be able to stand before the Son of Man. (LUKE 21:34–36 NCV)

Jesus said, Simon, Simon, behold, Satan has demanded permission to sift you like wheat; but I have prayed for you, that your faith may not fail; and you, when once you have turned again, strengthen your brothers. (LUKE 22:31–32 NASB)

But while Peter was in prison, the church prayed very earnestly for him. (ACTS 12:5 NLT)

We don't want you in the dark, friends, about how hard it was when all this came down on us in Asia province. It was so bad we didn't think we were going to make it. We felt like we'd been sent to death row, that it was all over for us. As it turned out, it was the best thing that could have happened. Instead of trusting in our own strength or wits to get out of it, we were forced to trust God totally—not a bad idea since he's the God who raises the dead! And he did it, rescued us from certain doom. And he'll do it again, rescuing us as many times as we need rescuing. You and your prayers are part of the rescue operation—I don't want you in the dark about that either. I can see your faces even now, lifted in praise for God's deliverance of us, a rescue in which your prayers played such a crucial part. **(2 CORINTHIANS 1:8–11 THE MESSAGE)**

Strength for the Journey

Prayer for Healing and Wholeness

There is no doubt that when Jesus walked the earth, the people who flocked to him everywhere he went begged for one thing more than any other: *healing*. They wanted what we all desire—to be well and whole, in body and mind; free of pain; and safe from wasting sicknesses that sap our strength and shorten our lives.

In our time we can no longer simply follow the crowds streaming into the countryside and hope for a chance to receive the Master's touch in person. But that doesn't mean healing is a thing of the past. God still delivers us from injury and illness, according to his will. Now we rely on prayer to make our request for wellness known to God—for ourselves and others.

As you will see in the following pages, when you have need of God's healing touch, the Bible urges you to pray with boldness, persistence, and—above all—steadfast faith.

David prayed for his son to be healed:

David pleaded with God for the child. He fasted and spent the nights lying in sackcloth on the ground. (2 SAMUEL 12:16 NIV)

And then this happened: Just as Jeroboam was at the Altar, about to make an offering, a holy man came from Judah by GOD's command and preached (these were GOD's orders) to the Altar: "Altar, Altar! GOD's message! 'A son will be born into David's family named Josiah. The priests from the shrines who are making offerings on you, he will sacrifice—on you! Human bones burned on you!'" At the same time he announced a sign: "This is the proof GOD gives—the Altar will split into pieces and the holy offerings spill into the dirt."

When the king heard the message the holy man preached against the Altar at Bethel, he reached out to grab him, yelling, "Arrest him!" But his arm was paralyzed and hung useless. At the same time the Altar broke apart and the holy offerings all spilled into the dirt—the very sign the holy man had announced by GOD's command.

The king pleaded with the holy man, "Help me! Pray to your GOD for the healing of my arm." The holy man prayed for him and the king's arm was healed—as good as new! (1 KINGS 13:1-6 THE MESSAGE)

In those days Hezekiah became sick and was at the point of death. And Isaiah the prophet the son of Amoz came to him and said to him, "Thus says the LORD, 'Set your house in order, for you shall die; you shall not recover.'" Then Hezekiah turned his face to the wall and prayed to the LORD, saying, "Now, O LORD, please remember how I have walked before you in faithfulness and with a whole heart, and have done what is good in your sight." And Hezekiah wept bitterly. And before Isaiah had gone out of the middle court, the word of the LORD came to him: "Turn back, and say to Hezekiah the leader of my people, Thus says the LORD, the God of David your father: I have heard your prayer; I have seen your tears. Behold, I will heal you. On the third day you shall go up to the house of the LORD, and I will add fifteen years to your life. I will deliver you and this city out of the hand of the king of Assyria, and I will defend this city for my own sake and for my servant David's sake." **(2 KINGS 20:1-6 ESV)**

In the midst of his suffering, Job's friend Elihu points out that God sometimes brings pain and illness to give a "wake-up call"—but can just as quickly provide complete healing.

Or, God might get their attention through pain,
by throwing them on a bed of suffering,
So they can't stand the sight of food,
have no appetite for their favorite treats.
They lose weight, wasting away to nothing,
reduced to a bag of bones.
They hang on the cliff-edge of death,
knowing the next breath may be their last.

73

But even then an angel could come,
    a champion—there are thousands of them!—
    to take up your cause,
A messenger who would mercifully intervene,
    canceling the death sentence with the words:
    "I've come up with the ransom!"
Before you know it, you're healed,
    the very picture of health! (JOB 33:19–25 THE
      MESSAGE)

O LORD my God, I cried out to You,
And You healed me.
O LORD, You brought my soul up from the
    grave;
You have kept me alive, that I should not go
    down to the pit. (PSALM 30:2–3 NKJV)

Heal me, O LORD, and I shall be healed;
Save me, and I shall be saved.
For You are my praise. (JEREMIAH 17:14 NKJV)

Then [Jesus] left the region of Tyre, went through Sidon back to Galilee Lake and over to the district of the Ten Towns. Some people brought a man who could neither hear nor speak and asked Jesus to lay a healing hand on him. He took the man off by himself, put his fingers in the man's ears and some spit on the man's tongue. Then Jesus looked up in prayer, groaned mightily, and commanded, "Ephphatha!—Open up!" And it happened. The man's hearing was clear and his speech plain—just like that. (MARK 7:31–35 THE MESSAGE)

Now there was at Joppa a disciple [a woman] named [in Aramaic] Tabitha, which [in Greek] means Dorcas. She was abounding in good deeds and acts of charity. About that time she fell sick and died, and when they had cleansed her, they laid [her] in an upper room. Since Lydda was near Joppa [however], the disciples, hearing that Peter was there, sent two men to him begging him, Do come to us without delay. So Peter [immediately] rose and accompanied them. And when he had arrived, they took him to the upper room. All the widows stood around him, crying and displaying undershirts (tunics) and [other] garments such as Dorcas was accustomed to make while she was with them. But Peter put them all out [of the room] and knelt down and prayed; then turning to the body he said, Tabitha, get up! And she opened her eyes; and when she saw Peter, she raised herself and sat upright. And he gave her his hand and lifted her up. Then calling in God's people and the widows, he presented her to them alive. (ACTS 9:36–41 AMP)

Luke recorded an account of a shipwreck he and Paul endured. They washed up on the shores of the island of Malta, where healings occurred.

The head man in that part of the island was Publius. He took us into his home as his guests, drying us out and putting us up in fine style for the next three days. Publius's father was sick at the time, down with a high fever and dysentery. Paul went to the old man's room, and when he laid hands on him and prayed, the man was healed. Word of the healing got around fast, and soon everyone on the island who was sick came and got healed. (ACTS 28:7–9 THE MESSAGE)

The apostle Paul wrote:

On behalf of this man I will boast, but on my own behalf I will not boast, except of my weaknesses—though if I should wish to boast, I would not be a fool, for I would be speaking the truth; but I refrain from it, so that no one may think more of me than he sees in me or hears from me. So to keep me from becoming conceited because of the surpassing greatness of the revelations, a thorn was given me in the flesh, a messenger of Satan to harass me, to keep me from becoming conceited. Three times I pleaded with the Lord about this, that it should leave me. But he said to me, "My grace is sufficient for you, for my power is made perfect in weakness." Therefore I will boast all the more gladly of my weaknesses, so that the power of Christ may rest upon me. For the sake of Christ, then, I am content with weaknesses, insults, hardships, persecutions, and calamities. For when I am weak, then I am strong. (2 CORINTHIANS 12:5–10 ESV)

Many people become discouraged or frustrated when God seemingly does not answer their prayers. But sometimes God's answer is actually "No" or "Not yet." Even Paul, one of the most influential believers of all time, did not receive the answer he wanted.

Is anyone among you sick? Let them call the elders of the church to pray over them and anoint them with oil in the name of the Lord. And the prayer offered in faith will make the sick person well; the Lord will raise them up. If they have sinned, they will be forgiven. Therefore confess your sins to each other and pray for each other so that you may be healed. The prayer of a righteous person is powerful and effective. (JAMES 5:14–16 NIV)

John, author of the fourth gospel, began a letter to his friend Gaius this way:

Dear friend, I pray that you may enjoy good health and that all may go well with you, even as your soul is getting along well. It gave me great joy when some believers came and testified about your faithfulness to the truth, telling how you continue to walk in it. (3 JOHN 1:2–3 NIV)

An Ally Amid Adversity

Prayer in Times of Hardship and Heartache

God knows very well when we face trying times and understands the limits of our endurance. When hardship and heartache have pushed you to the edge of your capacity to cope, he is by your side. Pray for strength and courage, and he'll be there to shore up your sagging defenses. Best of all, even in the asking you are not alone—for God's Word is here to show you how.

[Hannah] was deeply distressed and prayed to the LORD and wept bitterly. And she vowed a vow and said, "O LORD of hosts, if you will indeed look on the affliction of your servant and remember me and not forget your servant, but will give to your servant a son, then I will give him to the LORD all the days of his life" (1 SAMUEL 1:10–11 ESV).

Depend on the LORD and his strength;
    always go to him for help. (1 CHRONICLES 16:11
    NCV)

Answer me when I call to you,
    my righteous God.
Give me relief from my distress;
    have mercy on me and hear my prayer. (PSALM
    4:1 NIV)

Listen to my words, LORD,
consider my lament.
Hear my cry for help,
my King and my God,
for to you I pray. (PSALM 5:1–2 NIV)

The LORD is a shelter for the oppressed,
    a refuge in times of trouble.
Those who know your name trust in you,
    for you, O LORD, do not abandon those who
        search for you. (PSALM 9:9–10 NLT)

The Lord is King forever and ever;
    Destroy from your land those nations that do
        not worship you.
Lord, you have heard what the poor people
        want.
    Do what they ask, and listen to them.

Protect the orphans and put an end to suffering
   so they will no longer be afraid of evil people.
   (PSALM 10:16–18 NCV)

_____

The LORD will answer you in times of trouble.
   The name of the God of Jacob will protect
   you.
He will send you help from his holy place
   and support you from Zion. (PSALM 20:1–2
   GOD'S WORD)

_____

Turn to me and have mercy on me,
   because I am lonely and hurting.
My troubles have grown larger;
   free me from my problems. (PSALM 25:16–17
   NIV)

_____

I sought the LORD, and He answered me,
And delivered me from all my fears. (PSALM 34:4
   NASB)

_____

The righteous cry out, and the LORD hears,
and delivers them from all their troubles.
The LORD is near the brokenhearted;
He saves those crushed in spirit.

Many adversities come to the one who is
      righteous,
but the LORD delivers him from them all.
He protects all his bones;
   not one of them is broken. (PSALM 34:17–20 HCSB)

The LORD, the Mighty One, is God,
   and he has spoken. . . .
"Then call on me when you are in trouble,
   and I will rescue you,
   and you will give me glory." (PSALM 50:1, 15
   NLT)

Morning, noon, and night I am troubled and
   upset,
   but he will listen to me. (PSALM 55:17 NCV)

May my prayer come to you at an acceptable
   time, O LORD.
O God, out of the greatness of your mercy,
   answer me with the truth of your salvation.
Rescue me from the mud.
   Do not let me sink into it.
I want to be rescued from those who hate me
   and from the deep water. (PSALM 69:13–14 GOD'S
   WORD)

Then Jonah prayed to the LORD his God from the fish's belly.
And he said:

I cried out to the LORD because of my affliction,
And He answered me.

Out of the belly of Sheol I cried,
And You heard my voice.
For You cast me into the deep,
Into the heart of the seas,

And the floods surrounded me;
All Your billows and Your waves passed over me.
Then I said, "I have been cast out of Your sight;
Yet I will look again toward Your holy temple."
The waters surrounded me, even to my soul;
The deep closed around me;
Weeds were wrapped around my head.
I went down to the moorings of the mountains;
The earth with its bars closed behind me forever;
Yet You have brought up my life from the pit,
O LORD, my God.

When my soul fainted within me,
I remembered the LORD;
And my prayer went up to You,
Into Your holy temple. (JONAH 2:1-7 NKJV)

Prior to the Crucifixion, Jesus asked his Father for strength to carry out God's will, despite the excruciating pain he knew would come:

Then Jesus went with his followers to a place called Geth-semane. He said to them, "Sit here while I go over there and pray." He took Peter and the two sons of Zebedee with him, and he began to be very sad and troubled. He said to them, "My heart is full of sorrow, to the point of death. Stay here and watch with me."

After walking a little farther away from them, Jesus fell to the ground and prayed, "My Father, if it is possible, do not give me this cup of suffering. But do what you want, not what I want." Then Jesus went back to his followers and found them asleep. He said to Peter, "You men could not stay awake with me for one hour? Stay awake and pray for strength against temptation. The spirit wants to do what is right, but the body is weak."

Then Jesus went away a second time and prayed, "My Father, if it is not possible for this painful thing to be taken from me, and if I must do it, I pray that what you want will be done."

Then he went back to his followers, and again he found them asleep, because their eyes were heavy. So Jesus left them and went away and prayed a third time, saying the same thing. (MATTHEW 26:36–44 NCV)

Jesus said, Won't God give his chosen people justice when they cry out to him for help day and night? Is he slow to help them? I can guarantee that he will give them justice quickly. (LUKE 18:7–8 GOD'S WORD)

Be patient in trouble, and keep on praying. (ROMANS 12:12 NLT)

Do not be anxious about anything, but in everything by prayer and supplication with thanksgiving let your requests be made known to God. And the peace of God, which surpasses all understanding, will guard your hearts and your minds in Christ Jesus. (PHILIPPIANS 4:6–7 ESV)

The real widow, left all alone, has put her hope in God and continues night and day in her petitions and prayers. (1 TIMOTHY 5:5 HCSB)

During the days of Jesus' life on earth, he offered up prayers and petitions with fervent cries and tears to the one who could save him from death, and he was heard because of his reverent submission. (HEBREWS 5:7 NIV)

If any of you are having trouble, pray. (JAMES 5:13 GOD'S WORD)

Be humble under God's powerful hand so he will lift you up when the right time comes. Give all your worries to him, because he cares about you. (1 PETER 5:6–7 NCV)

A Bounty of Blessings

Prayer for Provision and Prosperity

Many people know instinctively to reach for prayer as a shield against misfortune—illness, financial ruin, natural disaster, and so on. Few, however, truly understand that prayer is more than a spiritual 911 call—to be used only in case of an emergency. God has offered us far more than disaster relief when we pray. He has promised to provide what we need to thrive in this life.

Prayer is our opportunity to trust in that promise and participate in his provision by boldly telling our Creator what we want and need. According to the Bible, *asking* is the key to *having,* so that we will remember where our prosperity originates—with God, and not in worldly systems and sources.

These verses will inspire you to hope for—and ask for—
more from your Father than you ever have before.

The skeptic swore, "There is no God! No
　　God!—I can do anything I want!
I'm more animal than human;
　　so-called human intelligence escapes me.

"I flunked 'wisdom.'
　　I see no evidence of a holy God.
Has anyone ever seen Anyone
　　climb into Heaven and take charge?
　　grab the winds and control them?
　　gather the rains in his bucket?
　　stake out the ends of the earth?
Just tell me his name, tell me the names of his
　　sons.
　　Come on now—tell me!"

The believer replied, "Every promise of God
　　proves true;
　　he protects everyone who runs to him for
　　help.
So don't second-guess him;
　　he might take you to task and show up your
　　lies."
And then he prayed, "God, I'm asking for two
　　things
　　before I die; don't refuse me—
Banish lies from my lips
　　and liars from my presence.

88

Give me enough food to live on,
    neither too much nor too little.
If I'm too full, I might get independent,
    saying, 'God? Who needs him?'
If I'm poor, I might steal
    and dishonor the name of my God."
        (PROVERBS 30:1–9 THE MESSAGE)

God told his people:

All my people will be blessed by the LORD.
They and their children will be blessed.
I will provide for their needs before they ask,
and I will help them while they are still asking
    for help. **(ISAIAH 65:23–24 NCV)**

For I know the plans I have for you, declares the LORD, plans for welfare and not for evil, to give you a future and a hope. Then you will call upon me and come and pray to me, and I will hear you. You will seek me and find me, when you seek me with all your heart. I will be found by you, declares the LORD, and I will restore your fortunes and gather you from all the nations and all the places where I have driven you, declares the LORD, and I will bring you back to the place from which I sent you into exile.

Because you have said, "The LORD has raised up prophets for us in Babylon" **(JEREMIAH 29:11–15 ESV).**

Jesus said, My command is this: Love each other as I have loved you. Greater love has no one than this: to lay down one's life for one's friends. You are my friends if you do what

I command. I no longer call you servants, because a servant does not know his master's business. Instead, I have called you friends, for everything that I learned from my Father I have made known to you. You did not choose me, but I chose you and appointed you so that you might go and bear fruit—fruit that will last—and so that whatever you ask in my name the Father will give you. This is my command: Love each other. (JOHN 15:12–17 NIV)

I'm glad in God, far happier than you would ever guess—happy that you're again showing such strong concern for me. Not that you ever quit praying and thinking about me. You just had no chance to show it. Actually, I don't have a sense of needing anything personally. I've learned by now to be quite content whatever my circumstances. I'm just as happy with little as with much, with much as with little. I've found the recipe for being happy whether full or hungry, hands full or hands empty. Whatever I have, wherever I am, I can make it through anything in the One who makes me who I am. I don't mean that your help didn't mean a lot to me—it did. It was a beautiful thing that you came alongside me in my troubles. (PHILIPPIANS 4:10–14 THE MESSAGE)

Because of this [the believers' faith in God and love for others], since the day we heard about you, we have continued praying for you, asking God that you will know fully what he wants. We pray that you will also have great wisdom and understanding in spiritual things so that you will live the kind of life that honors and pleases the Lord in every way. You will produce fruit in every good work and grow in the knowledge of God. (COLOSSIANS 1:9–10 NCV)

We pray very hard night and day that we may see you again so that we can supply whatever you still need for your faith. We pray that God our Father and the Lord Jesus will guide us to you. We also pray that the Lord will greatly increase your love for each other and for everyone else, just as we love you. Then he will strengthen you to be holy. Then you will be blameless in the presence of our God and Father when our Lord Jesus comes with all God's holy people. (1 THESSALONIANS 3:10-13 GOD'S WORD)

Because of his assurance of the faith among the believers at Thessalonica, the apostle Paul told them:

That is why we always pray for you, asking our God to help you live the kind of life he called you to live. We pray that with his power God will help you do the good things you want and perform the works that come from your faith. We pray all this so that the name of our Lord Jesus Christ will have glory in you, and you will have glory in him. That glory comes from the grace of our God and the Lord Jesus Christ. (2 THESSALONIANS 1:11-12 NCV)

Paul wrote to Philemon, his fellow servant in Christ:

I hear about your faithfulness to the Lord Jesus and your love for all of God's people. As you share the faith you have in common with others, I pray that you may come to have a complete knowledge of every blessing we have in Christ. Your love for God's people gives me a lot of joy and encouragement. You, brother, have comforted God's people. (PHILEMON 1:5-7 GOD'S WORD)

91

Give God the Glory

Prayer As Praise

Routine prayer for yourself is an excellent way to acknowledge your dependence on God and include him in all of life's perils and passages. Even more powerful is to pray for others, since mercy and compassion are potent multipliers of the effectiveness of prayer.

But, above all else, the prayers you offer up with the singular purpose of praising your magnificent and mighty Creator are supercharged with energy and have the capacity to unite you with him like nothing else. The issue isn't that he is more likely to listen when we praise him; the issue is that *we* are better able to grasp the incomparable good news of salvation when our eyes are fixed on him alone.

The following verses attest to this truth: Praise is the purest and most powerful of all our prayers.

Give thanks to the LORD and pray to him.
Tell the nations what he has done.
Sing to him; sing praises to him.
Tell about all his miracles.
Be glad that you are his;
let those who seek the LORD be happy. . . .
Remember the miracles he has done,
his wonders, his decisions. **(1 CHRONICLES 16:8–
10, 12 NCV)**

*David had called upon the people of Israel to give money and supplies
to build a temple to the Lord, and the people responded generously.*

King David was also overjoyed, and he praised the LORD
while the whole assembly watched. David said,

May you be praised, LORD God of Israel,
our father forever and ever.
Greatness, power, splendor, glory, and majesty
are yours, LORD,
because everything in heaven and on earth is
yours.
The kingdom is yours, LORD,
and you are honored as head of all things.
(1 CHRONICLES 29:9–11 GOD'S WORD)

The trumpeters and singers joined together to praise and
thank the LORD with one voice. They raised their voices, accompanied by trumpets, cymbals, and musical instruments,
in praise to the LORD:

For He is good;
His faithful love endures forever.

The temple, the LORD's temple, was filled with a cloud.
And because of the cloud, the priests were not able to continue
ministering, for the glory of the LORD filled God's temple.
(2 CHRONICLES 5:13–14 HCSB)

I will give thanks to the LORD with my whole
heart;
I will recount all of your wonderful deeds.
I will be glad and exult in you;
I will sing praise to your name, O Most High.
(PSALM 9:1–2 ESV)

God, you will be praised in Jerusalem.
We will keep our promises to you.
You hear our prayers.
All people will come to you. **(PSALM 65:1–2 NCV)**

Shout joyfully to God, all the earth;
Sing the glory of His name;
Make His praise glorious.
Say to God, "How awesome are Your works!
Because of the greatness of Your power Your en-
emies will give feigned obedience to You.

"All the earth will worship You,
And will sing praises to You;
They will sing praises to Your name." **(PSALM
66:1–4 NASB)**

Thanks be to God,
who has not rejected my prayer
or taken away his mercy from me. (PSALM
66:20 GOD'S WORD)

There is no one like You among the gods, O Lord,
Nor are there any works like Yours.
All nations whom You have made shall come
and worship before You, O Lord,
And they shall glorify Your name.
For You are great and do wondrous deeds;
You alone are God.

Teach me Your way, O LORD;
I will walk in Your truth;
Unite my heart to fear Your name.
I will give thanks to You, O Lord my God, with
all my heart,
And will glorify Your name forever.
For Your lovingkindness toward me is great,
And You have delivered my soul from the depths
of Sheol. (PSALM 86:8–13 NASB)

Praise the LORD.

Praise God in his sanctuary;
praise him in his mighty heavens.
Praise him for his acts of power;
praise him for his surpassing greatness.
Praise him with the sounding of the trumpet,
praise him with the harp and lyre,

praise him with timbrel and dancing,
praise him with the strings and pipe,
praise him with the clash of cymbals,
praise him with resounding cymbals.

Let everything that has breath praise the LORD.
(PSALM 150:1-6 NIV)

Mary responded to her cousin Elizabeth's enthusiastic greeting:

Oh, how my soul praises the Lord.
How my spirit rejoices in God my Savior!
For he took notice of his lowly servant girl,
and from now on all generations will call me
blessed.
For the Mighty One is holy,
and he has done great things for me.
He shows mercy from generation to generation
to all who fear him.
His mighty arm has done tremendous things!
He has scattered the proud and haughty
ones.
He has brought down princes from their thrones
and exalted the humble.
He has filled the hungry with good things
and sent the rich away with empty hands.
He has helped his servant Israel
and remembered to be merciful.
For he made this promise to our ancestors,
to Abraham and his children forever. **(LUKE
1:46-55 NLT)**

Zechariah praised God after the birth of John the Baptist:

Praise be to the Lord, the God of Israel,
 because he has come to his people and re-
 deemed them.
He has raised up a horn of salvation for us
 in the house of his servant David
(as he said through his holy prophets of long
 ago),
salvation from our enemies
 and from the hand of all who hate us—
to show mercy to our ancestors
 and to remember his holy covenant,
the oath he swore to our father Abraham:
to rescue us from the hand of our enemies,
 and to enable us to serve him without fear
in holiness and righteousness before him all our
 days. (LUKE 1:68–75 NIV)

All praise to the God and Father of our Master, Jesus the Messiah! Father of all mercy! God of all healing counsel! He comes alongside us when we go through hard times, and before you know it, he brings us alongside someone else who is going through hard times so that we can be there for that person just as God was there for us. (2 CORINTHIANS 1:3–4 THE MESSAGE)

Praise the God and Father of our Lord Jesus Christ, who has blessed us in Christ with every spiritual blessing in the heavens. (EPHESIANS 1:3 HCSB)

Praise be to the God and Father of our Lord Jesus Christ! In his great mercy he has given us new birth into a living hope through the resurrection of Jesus Christ from the dead, and into an inheritance that can never perish, spoil or fade. (1 PETER 1:3–4 NIV)

> Now to Him who is able to keep you from
>   stumbling,
> And to present you faultless
> Before the presence of His glory with exceeding
>   joy,
> To God our Savior,
> Who alone is wise,
> Be glory and majesty,
> Dominion and power,
> Both now and forever.
> Amen. (JUDE 1:24–25 NKJV)

Then I heard again what sounded like the shout of a vast crowd or the roar of mighty ocean waves or the crash of loud thunder:

> Praise the Lord!
>   For the Lord our God, the Almighty, reigns.
> Let us be glad and rejoice,
>   and let us give honor to him. (REVELATION
>   19:6–7 NLT)

Timeless Tutors

Biblical Prayers to Follow

Sooner or later, everyone who wants to make prayer a regular part of his or her life asks the question: *Am I doing this right?* It doesn't come naturally to anyone. The disciples themselves once boldly asked Jesus to teach them to pray—and thanks to that request we have the Lord's Prayer.

But while the Bible rarely offers step-by-step prayer instructions, its stories are filled with beautiful and moving *examples* we can learn from. The Psalms are a treasure trove of prayer templates for many occasions. Read the stirring and instructive prayers of Daniel, Hannah, Elijah, Stephen, Paul—even of Jesus himself when breaking bread to feed the multitudes, in the Garden of Gethsemane, and on the cross.

The words don't matter as much as the spirit of boldness and love that infuses them.

No matter where you are in your journey of prayer, follow in the footsteps of those who spoke to God in the pages of his Word.

Hannah's song of thanksgiving:

> My heart exults in the LORD;
> My horn is exalted in the LORD,
> My mouth speaks boldly against my enemies,
> Because I rejoice in Your salvation.
> There is no one holy like the LORD,
> Indeed, there is no one besides You,
> Nor is there any rock like our God.
> Boast no more so very proudly,
> Do not let arrogance come out of your mouth;
> For the LORD is a God of knowledge,
> And with Him actions are weighed.
> The bows of the mighty are shattered,
> But the feeble gird on strength.
> Those who were full hire themselves out for
>   bread,
> But those who were hungry cease to hunger.
> Even the barren gives birth to seven,
> But she who has many children languishes.
> The LORD kills and makes alive;
> He brings down to Sheol and raises up.
> The LORD makes poor and rich;
> He brings low, He also exalts.
> He raises the poor from the dust,

He lifts the needy from the ash heap
To make them sit with nobles,
And inherit a seat of honor;
For the pillars of the earth are the LORD's,
And He set the world on them.
He keeps the feet of His godly ones,
But the wicked ones are silenced in darkness;
For not by might shall a man prevail.
Those who contend with the LORD will be
    shattered;
Against them He will thunder in the heavens,
The LORD will judge the ends of the earth;
And He will give strength to His king,
And will exalt the horn of His anointed.

(1 SAMUEL 2:1–10 NASB)

King David's prayer of thanksgiving:

Lord God, who am I? What is my family? Why did you bring me to this point? But even this is not enough for you, Lord God. You have also made promises about my future family. This is extraordinary, Lord God.

What more can I say to you, Lord God, since you know me, your servant, so well! You have done this great thing because you said you would and because you wanted to, and you have let me know about it. This is why you are great, Lord God! There is no one like you. There is no God except you. We have heard all this ourselves! There is no nation like your people Israel. They are the only people on earth that God chose to be his own. You made your name well known. You did great and wonderful miracles for them. You went ahead of them and forced other nations and their gods out of the land. You freed your people from slavery in Egypt. You made the people of Israel your very own people forever, and, LORD, you are their God.

Now, LORD God, keep the promise forever that you made about my family and me, your servant. Do what you have said. Then you will be honored always, and people will say, "The LORD All-Powerful is God over Israel!" And the family of your servant David will continue before you.

LORD All-Powerful, the God of Israel, you have said to me, "I will make your family great." So I, your servant, am brave enough to pray to you. Lord God, you are God, and your words are true. And you have promised these good things to me, your servant. Please, bless my family. Let it continue before you always. Lord God, you have said so. With your blessing let my family always be blessed. (2 SAMUEL 7:18–29 NCV)

Solomon's prayer of dedication for the temple:

Then Solomon stood before the altar of the LORD in the presence of all the assembly of Israel and spread out his hands toward heaven, and said, "O LORD, God of Israel, there is no God like you, in heaven above or on earth beneath, keeping covenant and showing steadfast love to your servants who walk before you with all their heart; you have kept with your servant David my father what you declared to him. You spoke with your mouth, and with your hand have fulfilled it this day. Now therefore, O LORD, God of Israel, keep for your servant David my father what you have promised him, saying, 'You shall not lack a man to sit before me on the throne of Israel, if only your sons pay close attention to their way, to walk before me as you have walked before me.' Now therefore, O

God of Israel, let your word be confirmed, which you have spoken to your servant David my father.

"But will God indeed dwell on the earth? Behold, heaven and the highest heaven cannot contain you; how much less this house that I have built! Yet have regard to the prayer of your servant and to his plea, O LORD my God, listening to the cry and to the prayer that your servant prays before you this day, that your eyes may be open night and day toward this house, the place of which you have said, 'My name shall be there,' that you may listen to the prayer that your servant offers toward this place. And listen to the plea of your servant and of your people Israel, when they pray toward this place. And listen in heaven your dwelling place, and when you hear, forgive.

"If a man sins against his neighbor and is made to take an oath and comes and swears his oath before your altar in this house, then hear in heaven and act and judge your servants, condemning the guilty by bringing his conduct on his own head, and vindicating the righteous by rewarding him according to his righteousness. . . .

"Let your eyes be open to the plea of your servant and to the plea of your people Israel, giving ear to them whenever they call to you. For you separated them from among all the peoples of the earth to be your heritage, as you declared through Moses your servant, when you brought our fathers out of Egypt, O Lord God" (1 KINGS 8:1-32, 52-53 ESV).

Elijah's prayer at Mount Carmel, where the "contest" took place to see whose God was the one true God:

When it was time to offer the sacrifice, the prophet Elijah stepped forward. He said, "LORD God of Abraham, Isaac, and Israel, make known today that you are God in Israel and that I'm your servant and have done all these things by your instructions. Answer me, LORD! Answer me! Then these people will know that you, LORD, are God and that you are winning back their hearts."

So a fire from the LORD fell down and consumed the burnt offering, wood, stones, and dirt. The fire even dried up the water that was in the trench. All the people saw it and immediately bowed down to the ground. "The LORD is God!" they said. "The LORD is God!" (1 KINGS 18:36–39 GOD'S WORD).

The prayer of Jabez for a fruitful life:

Jabez cried out to the God of Israel, "Oh, that you would bless me and enlarge my territory! Let your hand be with me, and keep me from harm so that I will be free from pain." And God granted his request. (1 CHRONICLES 4:10 NIV)

The prophet Nehemiah was distressed about the poor condition of the wall surrounding Jerusalem, and he decided to initiate a rebuilding project. But first, he sought the Lord's favor and guidance:

O LORD, God of heaven, the great and awesome God who keeps his covenant of unfailing love with those who love him and obey his commands, listen to my prayer! Look down and see me praying night and day for your people Israel. I confess that we have sinned against you. Yes, even my own family and I have sinned! We have sinned terribly by not obeying the commands, decrees, and regulations that you gave us through your servant Moses.

Please remember what you told your servant Moses: "If you are unfaithful to me, I will scatter you among the nations.

But if you return to me and obey my commands and live by them, then even if you are exiled to the ends of the earth, I will bring you back to the place I have chosen for my name to be honored."

The people you rescued by your great power and strong hand are your servants. O Lord, please hear my prayer! Listen to the prayers of those of us who delight in honoring you. Please grant me success today by making the king favorable to me. Put it into his heart to be kind to me. (NEHEMIAH 1:5–11 NLT)

Daniel's prayer for his people:

It was the first year of the reign of Darius the Mede, the son of Ahasuerus, who became king of the Babylonians. During the first year of his reign, I, Daniel, learned from reading the word of the LORD, as revealed to Jeremiah the prophet, that Jerusalem must lie desolate for seventy years. So I turned to the LORD God and pleaded with him in prayer and fasting. I also wore rough burlap and sprinkled myself with ashes.

I prayed to the LORD my God and confessed:

"O Lord, you are a great and awesome God! You always fulfill your covenant and keep your promises of unfailing love to those who love you and obey your commands. But we have sinned and done wrong. We have rebelled against you and scorned your commands and regulations. We have refused to listen to your servants the prophets, who spoke on your authority to our kings and princes and ancestors and to all the people of the land.

"Lord, you are in the right; but as you see, our faces are covered with shame. This is true of all of us, including the people of Judah and Jerusalem and all Israel, scattered near and far, wherever you have driven us because of our disloyalty to you. O LORD, we and our kings, princes, and ancestors are covered with shame because we have sinned against you. But the Lord our God is merciful and forgiving, even though we have rebelled against him. We have not obeyed the LORD our God, for we have not followed the instructions he gave us through his servants the prophets. All Israel has disobeyed your instruction and turned away, refusing to listen to your voice. . . .

"O Lord our God, you brought lasting honor to your name by rescuing your people from Egypt in a great display of power. But we have sinned and are full of wickedness. In view of all your faithful mercies, Lord, please turn your furious anger away from your city Jerusalem, your holy mountain. All the neighboring nations mock Jerusalem and your people because of our sins and the sins of our ancestors.

"O our God, hear your servant's prayer! Listen as I plead. For your own sake, Lord, smile again on your desolate sanctuary.

"O my God, lean down and listen to me. Open your eyes and see our despair. See how your city—the city that bears your name—lies in ruins. We make this plea, not because we deserve help, but because of your mercy.

"O Lord, hear. O Lord, forgive. O Lord, listen and act! For your own sake, do not delay, O my God, for your people and your city bear your name" (DANIEL 9:1-11, 15-19 NLT).

The prophet Habukkuk's prayer of praise:

I have heard all about you, LORD.
  I am filled with awe by your amazing works.
In this time of our deep need,
  help us again as you did in years gone by.

And in your anger,
   remember your mercy.
I see God moving across the deserts from
   Edom,
   the Holy One coming from Mount Paran.
His brilliant splendor fills the heavens,
   and the earth is filled with his praise.
His coming is as brilliant as the sunrise.
   Rays of light flash from his hands,
   where his awesome power is hidden.
Pestilence marches before him;
   plague follows close behind.
When he stops, the earth shakes.
   When he looks, the nations tremble.
He shatters the everlasting mountains
   and levels the eternal hills.
   He is the Eternal One!
I see the people of Cushan in distress,
   and the nation of Midian trembling in terror.
Was it in anger, LORD, that you struck the rivers
   and parted the sea?
Were you displeased with them?
   No, you were sending your chariots of
      salvation!
You brandished your bow
   and your quiver of arrows.
   You split open the earth with flowing rivers.
The mountains watched and trembled.
   Onward swept the raging waters.
The mighty deep cried out,
   lifting its hands to the LORD. . . .

The Sovereign LORD is my strength!
He makes me as surefooted as a deer,
able to tread upon the heights. (HABAKKUK
3:2–10, 19 NLT)

Jesus' intercessory prayer, sometimes called "The High Priestly Prayer":

Jesus spoke these things; and lifting up His eyes to heaven, He said, "Father, the hour has come; glorify Your Son, that the Son may glorify You, even as You gave Him authority over all flesh, that to all whom You have given Him, He may give eternal life. This is eternal life, that they may know You, the only true God, and Jesus Christ whom You have sent. I glorified You on the earth, having accomplished the work which You have given Me to do. Now, Father, glorify Me together with Yourself, with the glory which I had with You before the world was.

"I have manifested Your name to the men whom You gave Me out of the world; they were Yours and You gave them to Me, and they have kept Your word. Now they have come to know that everything You have given Me is from You; for the words which You gave Me I have given to them; and they received them and truly understood that I came forth from You, and they believed that You sent Me. I ask on their behalf; I do not ask on behalf of the world, but of those whom You have given Me; for they are Yours; and all things that are Mine are Yours, and Yours are Mine; and I have been glorified in them. I am no longer in the world; and yet they themselves are in the world, and I come to You. Holy Father, keep them in Your name, the name which You have given Me, that they may be one even as We are. While I was with them, I was keeping them in Your name which You have given Me; and I guarded them and not one of them perished but the son of perdition, so that the Scripture would be fulfilled.

"But now I come to You; and these things I speak in the world so that they may have My joy made full in themselves. I have given them Your word; and the world has hated them, because they are not of the world, even as I am not of the world. I do not ask You to take them out of the world, but to keep them from the evil one. They are not of the world, even as I am not of the world. Sanctify them in the truth; Your word is truth. As You sent Me into the world, I also have sent them into the world. For their sakes I sanctify Myself, that they themselves also may be sanctified in truth.

"I do not ask on behalf of these alone, but for those also who believe in Me through their word; that they may all be one; even as You, Father, are in Me and I in You, that they also may be in Us, so that the world may believe that You sent Me.

"The glory which You have given Me I have given to them, that they may be one, just as We are one; I in them and You in Me, that they may be perfected in unity, so that the world may know that You sent Me, and loved them, even as You have loved Me. Father, I desire that they also, whom You have given Me, be with Me where I am, so that they may see My glory which You have given Me, for You loved Me before the foundation of the world.

"O righteous Father, although the world has not known You, yet I have known You; and these have known that You sent Me; and I have made Your name known to them, and will make it known, so that the love with which You loved Me may be in them, and I in them" (JOHN 17:1–26 NASB).

The early believers' prayer for courage:

As soon as they were freed, Peter and John returned to the other believers and told them what the leading priests and elders had said. When they heard the report, all the believers lifted their voices together in prayer to God: "O Sovereign Lord, Creator of heaven and earth, the sea, and everything in them—you spoke long ago by the Holy Spirit through our ancestor David, your servant, saying,

> Why were the nations so angry?
>   Why did they waste their time with futile
>   plans?
> The kings of the earth prepared for battle;
>   the rulers gathered together
> against the LORD
>   and against his Messiah.

"In fact, this has happened here in this very city! For Herod Antipas, Pontius Pilate the governor, the Gentiles, and the people of Israel were all united against Jesus, your holy servant, whom you anointed. But everything they did was determined beforehand according to your will. And now, O Lord, hear their threats, and give us, your servants, great boldness in preaching your word. Stretch out your hand with healing power; may miraculous signs and wonders be done through the name of your holy servant Jesus."

After this prayer, the meeting place shook, and they were all filled with the Holy Spirit. Then they preached the word of God with boldness. (ACTS 4:23–31 NLT)

Martyred for his faith, Stephen prayed as he was being killed:

When they had driven him out of the city, they began stoning him; and the witnesses laid aside their robes at the feet of a young man named Saul. They went on stoning Stephen as he called on the Lord and said, "Lord Jesus, receive my spirit!" Then falling on his knees, he cried out with a loud voice, "Lord, do not hold this sin against them!" Having said this, he fell asleep. (**ACTS 7:58–60 NASB**)

Paul assured the Ephesian believers of his prayers on their behalf:

For this reason, ever since I heard about your faith in the Lord Jesus and your love for all God's people, I have not stopped giving thanks for you, remembering you in my prayers. I keep asking that the God of our Lord Jesus Christ, the glorious Father, may give you the Spirit of wisdom and revelation, so that you may know him better. I pray that the eyes of your heart may be enlightened in order that you may know the hope to which he has called you, the riches of his glorious inheritance in his holy people, and his incomparably great power for us who believe. (**EPHESIANS 1:15–19 NIV**)

Paul asked God to provide spiritual power to the Ephesian believers:

For this reason I kneel before the Father from whom every family in heaven and on earth is named. I pray that He may grant you, according to the riches of His glory, to be strengthened with power in the inner man through His Spirit, and that the Messiah may dwell in your hearts through faith. I pray that you, being rooted and firmly established in love, may be able to comprehend with all the saints what is the length and width, height and depth of God's love, and to know the Messiah's love that surpasses knowledge, so you may be filled with all the fullness of God. (EPHESIANS 3:14–19 HCSB)

Paul prayed for partners in ministry:

I thank my God for all the memories I have of you. Every time I pray for all of you, I do it with joy. I can do this because of the partnership we've had with you in the Good News from the first day you believed until now. I'm convinced that God, who began this good work in you, will carry it through to completion on the day of Christ Jesus. You have a special place in my heart. So it's right for me to think this way about all of you. All of you are my partners. Together we share God's favor, whether I'm in prison or defending and confirming the truth of the Good News. God is my witness that, with all the compassion of Christ Jesus, I long to see every one of you.

I pray that your love will keep on growing because of your knowledge and insight. That way you will be able to determine what is best and be pure and blameless until the day of Christ. Jesus Christ will fill your lives with everything that God's approval produces. Your lives will then bring glory and praise to God. (PHILIPPIANS 1:3–11 GOD'S WORD)

Appendix

Thoughts on Prayer
by Classic Christian Writers

CHARLES SPURGEON (1834–1892)

───────── Pray the Promises of God ─────────

What is prayer but the promise pleaded? A promise is, so to speak, the raw material of prayer. Prayer irrigates the fields of life with the waters which are stored up in the reservoirs of promise. The promise is the power of prayer. We go to God, and we say to him, "Do as thou hast said. O Lord, here is thy word; we beseech thee fulfill it." Thus the promise is the bow by which we shoot the arrows of supplication. I like in my time of trouble to find a promise which exactly fits my need, and then to put my finger on it, and say, "Lord, this is thy word; I beseech thee to prove that it is so, by carrying it out in my case. I believe that this is thine own writing; and

I pray thee make it good to my faith." . . . It is a great thing to be driven to prayer by necessity; but it is a better thing to be drawn to it by the expectation which the promise arouses. Should we pray at all if God did not find us an occasion for praying, and then encourage us with gracious promises of an answer? (From *According to the Promise or The Lord's Method of Dealing With His Chosen People*, 1887)

WAIT ON THE LORD

It may seem an easy thing to wait, but it is one of the postures which a Christian soldier learns not without years of teaching. Marching and quick-marching are much easier to God's warriors than standing still. There are hours of perplexity when the most willing spirit, anxiously desirous to serve the Lord, knows not what part to take. Then what shall it do? Vex itself by despair? Fly back in cowardice, turn to the right hand in fear, or rush forward in presumption? No, but simply wait. *Wait in prayer,* however. Call upon God, and spread the case before him; tell him your difficulty, and plead his promise of aid. In dilemmas between one duty and another, it is sweet to be humble as a child, and *wait with simplicity of soul* upon the Lord. It is sure to be well with us when we feel and know our own folly, and are heartily willing to be guided by the will of God. But *wait in faith.* Express your unstaggering confidence in him; for unfaithful, untrusting waiting, is but an insult to the Lord. Believe that if he keep you tarrying even till midnight, yet he will come at the right time; the vision shall come and shall not tarry. *Wait in quiet patience,* not rebelling because you are under the affliction, but blessing your God for it. Never murmur against the second cause, as the children of Israel did against Moses; never wish you could go back to the world again, but accept the case as it is, and put it as it stands, simply and with your whole heart, without any self-will, into the hand of your covenant God. (From *Morning and Evening,* August 30 Morning Devotional)

———————— THE POWER OF SOLITARY PRAYER ————————

Dear friends, when we are tempted and desire to overcome, the best weapon is prayer. When you cannot use the sword and the shield, take to yourself the famous weapon of All-prayer. So your Saviour did. . . . Believer, especially in temptation, be much in solitary prayer. As private prayer is the key to open heaven, so is it the key to shut the gates of hell. As it is a shield to prevent, so is it the sword with which to fight against temptation. Family-prayer, social prayer, prayer in the Church, will not suffice, these are very precious, but the best beaten spice will smoke in your censer in your private devotions, where no ear hears but God. Betake yourselves to solitude if you would overcome. (From *Spurgeon's Sermons,* "Gethsemane" [No. 493], 1863)

D. L. MOODY (1837–1899)

———————— GOD HEARS OUR PLEAS ————————

If you call on God for deliverance and for victory over sin and every evil, God isn't going to turn a deaf ear to your call. I don't care how black your life has been, I don't care what your past record has been, I don't care how disobedient you have been, I don't care how you have back-slidden and wandered; if you really want to come back, God accepts the willing mind, God will hear your prayer, and answer. . . .

Only be sincere, and God will hear your cry. Mark you, there is a sham cry. Mothers understand that; they know when their children cry in earnest, or whether it is a sham cry. Let the child give a real cry of distress, and the mother will leave everything and fly to her child. I have been forty years in Christian work, and I have never known God to disappoint any man or woman who was in earnest about their soul's salvation. (From *Moody's Latest Sermons*, 1900)

NO TIME TO PRAY?

There is many a business man today who will tell you he has no time to pray: his business is so pressing that he cannot call his family around him, and ask God to bless them. He is so busy that he cannot ask God to keep him and them from the temptations of the present life—the temptations of every day. Business is so pressing I am reminded of the words of an old Methodist minister: "If you have so much business to attend to that you have no time to pray, depend upon it you have more business on hand than God ever intended you should have." But look at [Daniel]. He had the whole, or nearly the whole, of the king's business to attend to. He was Prime Minister, Secretary of State, and Secretary of the Treasury, all in one. He had to attend to all his own work; and to give an eye to the work of lots of other men. And yet he found time to pray: not just now and then, nor once in a way, not just when he happened to have a few moments to spare, mark you—but three times a day. (From *Bible Characters*, 1900)

────────────── UNITED IN PRAYER ──────────────

I remember when preaching on one occasion to an immense audience in the Agricultural Hall in London, a father and mother were in great distress about their absent son, who had given up God's ways and had wandered from his father's home to the wild bush of Australia. These poor parents asked the united prayers of that vast congregation for their son, and I suppose fully twenty thousand rose to the mercy-seat. It was ascertained afterward that at the very hour those prayers ascended from the audience in London, that young man was riding through the Australian bush to a town a day's ride from his camp. Something caused him to think of his home and his parents, and as he sat in the saddle, the Spirit of God descended upon him, and he was convicted of sin. Dismounting, he knelt down by his horse's side and prayed to God for forgiveness, and in a little while he was assured of conversion. When he reached the town, he wrote the good news to his delighted mother, and asked if they would receive him at home. The answer flashed along the cable beneath the ocean—

"Come home at once."

So afraid were they that he might arrive in the night when they were not awake to receive him, that they fastened a big bell to the door, so that all the family would be awakened as he entered. (From *Pleasure and Profit in Bible Study and Anecdotes, Incidents and Illustrations*, 1915)

ANDREW MURRAY (1828–1917)

MEDITATION AND PRAYER

Meditation must lead to prayer. It provides matter for prayer. It must lead on to prayer, to ask and receive definitely what it has seen in the Word or accepted in the Word. Its value is that it is the preparation for prayer, deliberate and whole-hearted supplication for what the heart has felt that the Word has revealed as needful or possible. . . .

The reward of resting for a time from intellectual effort, and cultivating the habit of holy meditation, will be that in course of time the two will be brought into harmony, and all our study be animated by the spirit of a quiet waiting on God, and a yielding up of the heart and life to the Word.

Our fellowship with God is meant for all the day. The blessing of securing a habit of true meditation in the morning watch will be, that we shall be brought nearer the blessedness of the man of the first Psalm; "Blessed is the man [whose] . . . delight is in the law of the Lord, and in his law doth he meditate day and night." . . .

"Let the words of my mouth, and the meditation of my heart, be acceptable in Thy sight, O Lord, my Strength, and my Redeemer." Let nothing less be your aim—that your meditation may be acceptable in His sight—part of the spiritual sacrifice you offer. Let nothing less be your prayer and expectation, that your meditation may be true worship, the living surrender of the heart to God's Word in His presence. (From *The Inner Chamber and the Inner Life*, "Meditation," 1905)

——————————— PERSEVERING PRAYER ———————————

One of the greatest drawbacks to the life of prayer is the fact that the answer does not come as speedily as we expect. We are discouraged by the thought: "Perhaps I do not pray aright," and so we do not persevere in prayer. This was a lesson that our Lord taught often and urgently. If we consider the matter, we can see that there may be a reason for the delay, and the waiting may bring a blessing to our souls. Our desire must grow deeper and stronger, and we must ask with our whole heart. God puts us into the practicing school of persevering prayer that our weak faith may be strengthened. Do believe that there is a great blessing in the delayed answer to prayer.

Above all, God would draw us into closer fellowship with Himself. When our prayers are not answered, we learn to realize that the fellowship and nearness and love of God are more to us than the answers of our petitions, and we continue in prayer. . . .

Christians, listen to this warning. Be not impatient or discouraged if the answer does not come. Continue in prayer. "Pray without ceasing." You will find it an unspeakable blessing to do so. You will ask whether your prayer is really in accordance with the will of God and the Word of God. You will inquire if it is in the right spirit and in the Name of Christ. Keep on praying—you will learn that the delay in the answer to prayer is one of the most precious means of grace that God can bestow on you. You will learn, too, that those who have persevered often and long before God, in pleading His promises, are those who have had the greatest power with God in prayer. (From *God's Best Secrets*, 1923)

——————————— PRAYER AND GOD'S WORD ———————————

Prayer and the Word are inseparably linked together. Power in the use of either depends upon the presence of the other. The Word gives me matter for prayer, telling me what God will do for me. It shows me the path of prayer, telling me how God would have me come. It gives me the power for prayer, the courage of the assurance I will be heard. And it brings me the answer to prayer, as it teaches what God will do for me. And so, on the other hand, prayer prepares the heart for receiving the Word from God Himself, for the teaching of the Spirit to give the spiritual understanding of it, for the faith that is made partaker of its mighty working.

It is clear why this is so. Prayer and the Word have one common center—God. Prayer seeks God: the Word reveals God. In prayer man asks God: in the Word God answers man. In prayer man rises to heaven to dwell with God: in the Word God comes to dwell with man. In prayer man gives himself to God: in the Word God gives Himself to man. . . .

Prayer and the Word will be a blessed fellowship with God, the interchange of thought, and love and life: a dwelling in God and God in us. Seek God and live! (From *The Inner Chamber and the Inner Life*, "Moses and the Word of God," 1905)

F. B. MEYER (1847–1929)

―――――― PRAY CONFIDENTLY . . . AND TRUST GOD ――――――

In prayer, there must be deliberateness, the secret place, the inner chamber, the fixed time, the shut door against distraction and intruders. In that secret place the Father is waiting for us. He is as certainly there as He is in Heaven. Be reverent, as Moses when he took the shoes from off his feet! Be trustful, because you are having an audience with One who is infinite sympathy and love! Be comforted, because there is no problem He cannot solve, no knot He cannot untie!

God knows even better than we do what we need and should ask for. . . . You may be sure that, in some way or other, your Heavenly Father is going to meet your particular need. . . . When you have once definitely put a matter into God's hands, leave it there. (From *Our Daily Walk: Daily Meditations and a Prayer for Each Day*, March 6, "The Secret Place of Prayer")

―――――――――――― "TEACH US TO PRAY" ――――――――――――

Our Lord was not always insisting on prayer, but was constantly praying to His Father Himself. His disciples knew His habit of getting away for secret prayer, and they had on more than one occasion seen the transfiguring glory reflected on His face. Happy would it be for us if the glory of fellowship and communion with God were so apparent that men would come to us saying, "Teach us to pray" (EXODUS 34:35).

Prayer must be simple. The Jewish proverb said, "Everyone who multiplies prayer is heard," but our Lord forbade senseless repetition by His teaching of the simple, direct, and intelligible petitions of [the Lord's prayer].

Prayer must be reverent. The tenderest words, the simplest confidences, and closest intimacy will be welcomed and reciprocated by our Father in Heaven. But we must remember that He is the great King, and His name is Holy. Angels veil their faces in His Presence. Let us remember that "God is in heaven, and thou upon earth: be not rash with thy mouth, and let not thine heart be hasty to utter anything before God" [see ECCLESIASTES 5:2 KJV].

Prayer must be unselfish. Our Lord so wove intercession into the structure of this Prayer that none can use it without pleading for others. Sorrow or sin may isolate us and make us feel our loneliness and solitude, but in prayer we realize that we are members of the one Body of Christ. . . .

Prayer must deal with real needs. Daily bread stands for every kind of need, and the fact that Jesus taught us to pray for it, suggests that we may be sure that it is God's will to give.

Prayer must be in faith. We cannot but believe that we are as certain to prevail with God, as the good man of the house with his friend; and if among men to ask is to get, how much more with Him who loves us with more than a father's love (LUKE 11:9-13). (From *Our Daily Walk: Daily Meditations and a Prayer for Each Day*, March 7, "The Model Prayer")

R. A. TORREY (1856–1928)

———— INTERCESSION: A MINISTRY FOR ALL ————

This ministry of intercession is a glorious and a mighty ministry, and we can all have part in it. The man or the woman who is shut away from the public meetings by sickness can have part in it; the busy mother; the woman who has to take in washing for a living can have part—she can mingle prayers for the saints, and for her pastor, and for the unsaved, and for foreign missionaries, with the soap and water as she bends over the washtub, and not do the washing any more poorly on that account; the hard driven man of business can have part in it, praying as he hurries from duty to duty. But of course we must, if we would maintain this spirit of constant prayer, take time—and plenty of it—when we shall shut ourselves up in the secret place alone with God for nothing but prayer. (From *How to Pray*, 1900)

———————— PRAYER LEADS TO JOY ————————

Who is there that does not wish his joy filled full? Well, the way to have it filled full is by praying in the name of Jesus. We all know people whose joy is filled full, indeed, it is just running over, shining from their eyes, bubbling out of their very lips, and running off their fingertips when they shake hands with you. Coming in contact with them is like coming in contact with an electrical machine charged with gladness. Now people of that sort are always people that spend much time in prayer.

125

Why is it that prayer in the name of Christ brings such fullness of joy? In part, because we get what we ask. But that is not the only reason, nor the greatest. It makes God real. When we ask something definite of God, and He gives it, how real God becomes! He is right there! It is blessed to have a God who is real, and not merely an idea. I remember how once I was taken suddenly and seriously sick all alone in my study. I dropped upon my knees and cried to God for help. Instantly all pain left me—I was perfectly well. It seemed as if God stood right there, and had put out His hand and touched me. The joy of the healing was not so great as the joy of meeting God.

There is no greater joy on earth or in heaven, than communion with God, and prayer in the name of Jesus brings us into communion with Him. The psalmist was surely not speaking only of future blessedness, but also of present blessedness when he said, "In thy presence is fullness of joy" **(PSALM 16:11 KJV)**. (From *How to Pray*, 1900)

More Insight from God's Word

Have you ever wanted to ask God what heaven is like? It turns out, he's already told us! The Bible is filled with passages that describe it. In this book, you will find all the scriptural references to heaven, as well as brief, clear explanations from trustworthy commentaries.

Everything the Bible Says About Heaven

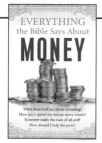

How people deal with money matters to God. In this short volume, all the scriptural references to money have been collected and explained in a clear and concise format. Hear what God has to say about everything related to money, including working, saving, tithing—and more!

Everything the Bible Says About Money

Supernatural beings—both the good and bad—fascinate us because they are surrounded by mystery. This book includes every Scripture passage relating to angels and demons along with brief commentaries to help you develop a clear, biblical point of view.

Everything the Bible Says About Angels and Demons

🕮 BETHANYHOUSE

Stay up-to-date on your favorite books and authors with our *free* e-newsletters. Sign up today at bethanyhouse.com.

Find us on Facebook.